Tales

From the Tarmac

REVISION

An astonishing 'behind the scenes' anthology of true
cases about passengers and ground staff at airports
worldwide

Claudia Helena Oxee

CONTENTS

Dedication

I personally devote this literary endeavor to you, my beloved daughter Lara, and to my four precious grandchildren.

Lara, you are the kindest daughter a mother could ever wish for. You'll never realize how much your incredible inner strength has influenced my personal growth. From the first moment I held you in my arms, it was *you* who gave me purpose and encouragement throughout all the years. You are amazing, and so loved, as are Sal, Aleah, Hunter and Tyler! You all give me such pride and joy!

Acknowledgement

As Claudia stated, without the generous literary contributions from everyone in Part Two and without the passengers who made her career so memorable, Tales From The Tarmac would be non-existent. Her ability to handle everything from routine operations to high-profile events--plus having an understanding of people--all come together in this book, offering readers an insider's view of airport life behind closed doors and far beyond "Do Not Enter!"

As she once succinctly pointed out,

"The measure of intelligence is the ability to change."

Albert Einstein.

This simple quote gave Claudia the impetus to recognize that our mindsets change accordingly over time and that every aspect of our lives necessitates reflection—That was her inspiration for the book's revision. Enjoy!

About the Author

Claudia Helena Oxee, along with her colleagues, was no stranger to chaos and complexity. She pulls back the curtain of hidden layers behind airport operations, offering readers an entertaining and eye-opening look at the inner workings of the aviation world. While airports may seem impersonal, Oxee shows they are filled with human emotions as she and the ground staff showcase their resilience and compassion. Claudia brings a unique, first-hand perspective to *Tales From the Tarmac*, infusing each story with the depth, humor and emotional resonance that can only come from someone who has lived these experiences. You'll laugh, gasp and possibly even tear up as you dive into this emotional rollercoaster of human encounters in one of the most high-stakes environments on the planet.

If you have any questions, feedback, or would like to share your thoughts about the book, feel free to reach out to:

TFTTreply@gmail.com

INTRODUCTION

By Claudia Oxee

The customary book inscription is analogous to personal gratitude for those whose encouragement is a contributing factor to the book's success.

I think we all basically know that working with the public can be rewarding or disturbing especially at airports. Dealing with the diversity and cultures of passengers surely had its challenges and these challenges gave me the impetus, along with my airline colleagues, to share some of our grandeur and lunacy with you.

To everyone who graciously tendered their time and their ubiquitous encounters, I attribute this audiobook to you because you were the inspiration for Tales from the Tarmac.

So, who am I? This brief introductory comes into play throughout the book.

In the mid 1980's, I answered a newspaper ad for a position with an international airline. I knew that would be my foot in the door, and come hell or high water, I was going to begin my desired career. I relinquished my then-lucrative full-time job as a fur model in New York City and traded in the furs for a uniform and the runways for jetways.

For many years I had the privilege of working at JFK Airport. My initiation as a neophyte began with TWA and PAN American Airways. Eventually, with internal connections and encouragement from PAN AM upper management, they arranged an interview for me with a fine German airline called LTU International Airways. The position of Station Manager was disclosed only via word of mouth since this is the norm at most airports. The interview worked in my favor and within a week, I was on my way to Germany for a month's schooling at their Headquarters in Dusseldorf. Since I was born in Germany, it was also to my advantage, affording me the opportunity to spend weekends with family while in training.

LTU's German translation was *Luft Transport Unternehmen*. LTU's English translation was simply *Air Transport Company*. However, there wasn't anything simple about it. LTU distinguished itself as an international leisure carrier since 1955 until it ceased operations in 2010. They were an immediate success due to the private financial backers and their extensive fleet of aircraft types.

Unlike most other carriers whose routes were mainly into capital cities, LTU's destinations were to exotic seacoast cities worldwide. In 1972 they commenced service into JFK Airport. Now granted, I think we can all agree that JFK in Jamaica, New York is not exactly an exotic seacoast. However, it was a very lucrative route during the summer seasons with load factors of approximately 408 passengers per flight via their long-range fleet of L-1011 aircraft.

After the initial month's training in Germany and enroute back to New York, trepidation and second thoughts weighed heavily on my mind since I was responsible for the JFK operation. This entailed, in part, making logical and immediate judgment calls whenever necessary. I had no one above me, so when major issues arose, the protocol was to call my superiors at Flight Operations in Germany which was manned 24/7, as are all airline Operations worldwide. Nonetheless the commitment and the challenges were frightening.

Since LTU was a sub-leaser at JFK, we required a handling agent. Fortunately, upper LTU management at HQ contracted KLM, the Royal Dutch Airlines. Their staff was always most professional, most courteous and a hell of a lot of fun, I might add. They were and still are an outstanding airline.

There were many perks that came with my job description, and hiring good assistants was at the top of the list. I did, and they were, as were all the wonderful LTU staff worldwide throughout the years. I also had the privilege of hiring my daughter Lara for a few summer seasons. It was such a special treat for me, and for Lara, it was a radical eye-opener to the behind-the-scenes matters of running an international carrier.

In 2011, while giving birth to the first Tales From The Tarmac in paperback, my beloved husband Jack who has since passed away, admirably championed my literary adventure down memory lane with his love and support. His extensive Ad-man expertise was most helpful, as were his candid critiques. We spent many memorable nights with pen and wine in hand.

For the second half of the book, I prevailed upon my endearing friends and colleagues in the industry to regale us with some of their stranger-than-fiction episodes. And as our stories unfold, perhaps you may recognize yourself as one of the cast members.

In essence, I am so grateful to everyone who was destined to share a paralleled path with me while my JFK journey ran its amazing course.

So please sit back, relax and enjoy our tales, ranging from the heart-throbbing to the heart-wrenching and from the ridiculous to the sublime.

TARMAC

A paved surface that withstands the weight of aircrafts for all ground operations such as taxiing, take-offs, landings, ramp usage, parking gates etc.

Chapter 1

Unforgettable

For airline staff, the summer months at any airport are demanding due to the upsurge of passengers and rigorous scheduling. At times, agents must work several flights simultaneously and are often pulled in many directions.

My first JFK job was for TWA in the International Terminal as a newbie. My position was that of a white-jacket employee, better known as a glorified gopher. My social life, or lack of it, required major adjustments since working weekends and holidays had become a part of my new norm. Eventually, as acceptance overrode ambiguity, the transition became tolerable. I was very low on the totem pole both salary and schedule-wise, but that was okay because for the first time, I was working where I wanted to be, and that was at JFK Airport.

TWA was a great airline for many reasons. One being that it afforded me the opportunity to climb that proverbial ladder. My attitude was that I had almost forty years of life experience...that should've counted for something, and that wisdom comes with age, so I thought! I had been a seasoned traveler most of my life, taught school in Vienna, Austria, where my daughter and I lived for a while, had a hectic lifestyle working in New York City for seven years, and raised a wonderful daughter in the face of extreme marital adversities.

I was also quite altruistic since my glass was always half-full in lieu of half-empty. Yet, the insecurities of beginning a new career were overwhelming especially since my former modeling salary plummeted down by several hundred dollars per week. My TWA salary was $6.75 per hour and that alone was a frightening reality. Also, I was now working at one of the world's most scrupulous airports, not as a passenger this time, but rather servicing them.

I often speak about the importance of fulfilling one's dreams in life because many of mine never came to fruition for reasons beyond my control. One such passion was aviation; to sit in the left chair in a cockpit, that was my ultimate dream. It was short-lived however, because my vision in both eyes was very poor and the rest is self-explanatory. Let's face it, flight training is just not given in Braille. So that dream literally never took flight, and sadly, neither did I.

My first day at TWA was awkward as any new job would be. My confidence tanked and I felt invisible. I tried to be perky, basically just kiss ass and smile. After training, our instructor stressed the importance of wearing practical shoes since comfort, not vanity, was a necessity. Did I listen? Well, of course not. After only two hours of wearing new shoes, both my feet had blisters like cherry tomatoes. They burnt and were literally fused to my pantyhose. It was mistakenly and painstakingly… are you ready? The *agony of de-feet*, both ways, I might add!

While passing a gate that was deplaning a flight, I noticed a little adorable white-haired man sitting in a wheelchair. It struck me odd that he was left alone having been taught that when wheelchair passengers are unaccompanied, they're usually positioned near an agent for their ground-time duration. This passenger was in transit from Cleveland, Ohio, after visiting family and returning to Italy via JFK. The designated meet-and-assist agent who initially took him off the jetway, placed him in the corner by himself near a men's room. Thinking that the agent was going to return and complete his assignment, I walked away and went over to mine. However, an hour later as I returned, there he was, still by himself, tucked in the corner. As I passed him, he politely smiled, so I dismissed my concerns considering he didn't appear to be in any notable distress.

TWA International Terminal was extremely chaotic that sweltering summer afternoon. I was constantly being pulled from one gate to another. While quickly walking to my Tel Aviv assignment, peripherally I saw the man still perched near the bathroom and that upset me. I approached his wheelchair and realized he spoke only Italian. Softly, he began sobbing and reached for my hands begging for help. I held his and assured him that I would. After retrieving documents from his front shirt pocket, it was apparent that he was a transiting passenger. Due to the negligence of the meet-and-assist agent, this passenger missed his Rome flight that had departed two hours earlier and no one had bothered looking for him. It was obvious that the Rome gate agents did not have a gate-check since the passenger had never boarded his flight to Italy. He was alone and completely defenseless. This was also a major security breach since his bags had been transferred from the Ohio flight to the Rome flight without him. In lieu of carrying out my Tel Aviv assignment, I consoled this sweet little man via hand gestures and attempted to calm his anxiety by radioing for assistance.

Twenty minutes later, a supervisor marched over and displayed annoyance towards me. Being my first day, I was perplexed as to why. What had I done wrong? Was it a Cardinal sin to ask for help for a TWA passenger? I expressed my contempt not only towards the situation but also towards the agent who left this man sitting all by himself. Thinking that she'd be somewhat empathetic, no, she just turned on her radio and said, "wheelchair passenger, bathroom assistance required, gate whatever", and that was it. Before walking away, she turned around and blatantly dismissed me.

Well, the 747 Tel Aviv flight finished boarding. The gate agents were maniacally scrambling to get a successful gate-check. Since no one had advised me of my next assignment, I took advantage of the situation and found a concession because my oozing blisters were analogous to firecrackers detonating on my feet. I needed to get Band-Aids immediately. I hobbled over to the ladies' room, slowly peeled off my pantyhose and placed the Band-Aids over the open sores. Oh, how I desperately wished I had orthopedic shoes at that moment!

Fast forward three hours later: there he still sat near the bathroom. My heart broke for him. I approached his wheelchair now for the fourth time and knelt at eye level out of respect and compassion while holding his hands. His eyes again filled with tears.

Whatever the consequences were at that point in time, it didn't matter. It was my mission to get him on a flight back to Italy that night. Immediately the adrenaline started flowing and my silly, self-inflicted flesh wounds became secondary.

First, I wheeled my buddy into the TWA commissary and explained the inhumane experience that this passenger had been subjected to, and a hot meal was on its way for him. From there, the same kind-hearted TWA agent checked the computer and found a flight leaving that night on Alitalia with a connection in the morning to his hometown. Since I wouldn't let him out of my sight not even for a moment, the agent arranged for an auto-link transfer for us to the Alitalia terminal.

Upon arrival, I carefully wheeled him in and asked for the Station Manager because I wanted to request an upgrade, considering the horrendous ordeal he had endured. She was appalled by the incident and cordially complied. She spoke to him in Italian and reassured him that while he was airborne, his family would be notified, and they'd be at the airport upon his arrival.

Under those circumstances, his TWA tickets were accepted at face value. I also asked her if I could bring my new buddy onboard the aircraft and personally secure him in his seatbelt, cover him with blankets, prop up his pillows and demonstrate all the mechanical goodies on his business class seat. We both spoke to him in a universal language that he understood... compassion. I then advised the in-flight purser of his many hours of torment as he sat alone helplessly and forgotten outside of the TWA bathroom. When all was said and done and it was time for me to exit the Alitalia aircraft, I knelt beside him again and gave him a big hug. He squeezed my hands tightly and placed them on his heart, and once again his eyes filled with tears. However, this time they were tears of joy rolling down his sweet little face as he expressed immeasurable gratitude in lieu of disparaging solitude.

After finishing my shift that night, I slowly walked out to the TWA ground-crew bus barefoot with shoes in hand, and I ostracized myself for doing something so stupid by wearing a new pair of heels, knowing that the job entailed continuous walking for eight hours. Then, my thoughts turned to the sweet little man who experienced such anguish due to sheer negligence for so many hours.

Fortunately, with the collective help of TWA and Alitalia, we managed to bring a heartfelt smile to this sweet man... a smile that was simply *unforgettable!*

Chapter 2

Down the Aisle

This story takes place in the former PAN AM Worldport at JFK.

To properly convey the following scenario, I'd like to preface this story by paraphrasing Sophia Petrillo's illustrious words from the hit television show, *The Golden Girls.*

As she used to say, "Picture this: afternoon shift, busy PAN AM departure gate, full 747, JFK/London flight… Got the picture?"

As I promptly made the pre-boarding announcement, sprinting towards the busy gate from way across the terminal, knocking down almost everything in their path were a bride and groom dressed in their complete wedding attire, yelling, wait, wait, we're here, wait!

The bride's loud voice was a spine-tingler and as the newlyweds approached the gate, their faces were all red and they were huffing and puffing and almost blew us all down…well, not really. Both were calorically challenged or as they say in today's vernacular, passengers of size. (Don't blame me please)

She was in her beautiful poofy gown and veil, and the groom was handsomely decked out in his tuxedo. He was sweating profusely while pulling both their oversized carry-ons.

We sincerely congratulated the happy couple and told them to relax as we pointed to the restrooms so they could change into comfortable traveling clothes. Well, the blushing bride wouldn't hear of it. She ignored our invitation to change and vehemently declared that it was their wedding day *and* night.

My colleagues and I tried to discourage this lunacy since it was not only a discomfort for them but also a safety issue for all passengers and crew. Our diplomatic attempts to dissuade them fell on deaf ears. The tenacious bride then took it even one step further by insisting on an upgrade stating that they were entitled to it. *How silly!*

I pulled up their reservation on the computer even though this was disruptive because boarding had already begun. Based on their record locator, the bride had purchased very low fares many months prior, assuming since it was their wedding day *and* night, who would be so heartless as to *not* bump them up to first class.

Now, under any other circumstances, we certainly would have done so however, the new little Mrs. was just straight-out bitchy. We told her to take a seat since upgrades were based on, among other things, the load factors once boarding had been completed. This is standard procedure. Five minutes later, she came back up to the podium and demanded the upgrades while using locker room profanity.

During the boarding process, and I think you can all relate, it's always hectic anyway as passengers start asking redundant questions not realizing that time is of the essence to get an on-time departure.

After a few more insulting obscenities, the sewer-mouthed bride made the decision for us... *absolutely* no upgrade. When we told her zero, nada, nix, nein and no, she was incensed and used the F-word once too often. She loudly proclaimed that she will never fly on this F-ing airline again. Our silent reaction to that was… whew, do you promise? Unbeknownst to her and her hen-pecked husband who sat there and hardly said a word, we did block two extra seats for them and isolated their stupidity to the rear of the aircraft.

When all the passengers were onboard, they then stomped up the jetway with the groom balancing her bridal train in one hand and the carry-ons in the other. It was truly a cartoon scene. I immediately followed them to advise the in-flight purser of a gate-check and of the bridezilla's behavior.

Most airlines acknowledge nuptials with courtesy upgrades when possible and complimentary champagne. I think we can all form a visual of this disgruntled couple as they walked down the aisle to the rear of the cabin.

After the aircraft pushed back from the gate, we gate agents were thoroughly perplexed at the less-than-pragmatic decision these foolish newlyweds made.

We wondered; how would they be able to sit on a six-hour trans-Atlantic flight fully consumed by their wedding attire…. I mean talk about chafing and sweaty balls! And how would they indulge in their undeniably favorite pastime of eating? Another crude and unpleasant visual was that of the bodacious bride using the tiny toilets and how in Heaven's name would she negotiate the proverbial wipe?

Their first walk down the aisle that day was in a church happily exchanging I dos. Their second walk down the aisle that day was in a PAN AM aircraft angrily exchanging outbursts.

Despite the belligerence and disrespect toward us all, my colleagues and I arranged for a complimentary bottle of champagne to be gifted to them during their extremely uncomfortable flight. Between their two extra seats and the bubbly, PAN AM did acknowledge their wedding day *and* night.

We were all also curious as to the reaction of the PAN AM gate agents that were meeting the flight on the other side of the pond as they landed at London's Heathrow Airport. Now wouldn't that have been interesting to see? This entire craziness begged the question, what were these airheads thinking?

So there you have it boys and girls, one of many stranger-than-fiction tales from the tarmac.

Chapter 3

The Bombing of PAN AM Flight 103 Over Lockerbie, Scotland

December 21, 1988... a day in aviation infamy that will forever remain enmeshed in the hearts of mankind!

The Christmas season for me had already been plagued with the upheaval of a seven-year relationship that was meeting its demise. Weight loss, insomnia, depression and loneliness amidst the holiday festivities were my precursors to the initial stages of the mourning process. I had never experienced such emotional numbness, and my daily functionality was robotic at best. I had been *jilted*. Working at PAN AM's Worldport afforded me a few hours of soul-stirring relief since it entailed afternoon and evening shifts with bustling holiday travelers that kept me immersed in work.

The day began as usual with a 2:30 p.m. briefing, which consisted of PAN AM's daily flight movements. My usual assignment was working a gate that operated three simultaneous flights and after the briefing, my colleagues and I went to gate 24/25/26.

It was already deluged with long queues of anxious holiday travelers. At approximately 4:00 p.m., amid the hectic workload, two PAN AM VIPs whom I had known approached the gate and asked me to bring my belongings and follow them. Their mood was somber and my immediate reaction was that I had been terminated since my pensive disposition was obviously apparent. Enroute to one of their private offices not a word was spoken until we were all behind closed doors.

It was then that my personal pain transcended into grief unlike anything I had ever experienced. I was advised that PAN AM Flight 103 had crashed shortly after take-off from London's Heathrow Airport. Accurate details had not yet been determined other than the 747 Jumbo jet touched down at Heathrow Airport at noon (GMT) from San Francisco, California. The aircraft was routinely cleaned, catered, fueled and bags were off/onloaded during the two-hour turnaround on the tarmac. The 747 was guarded by PAN AM's own security company by the name of Alert Security. This company proved to be disastrous since their employees at Frankfurt airport in Germany, where the first leg of the flight originated, had no formal security training. Upon landing at Heathrow, these Frankfurt passengers transited to the awaiting Flight 103. They boarded the aircraft along with the additional passengers who were heading home for the holidays to New York's JFK airport.

I was advised that a possible mechanical brought down *'Clipper Maid* of the Seas' over the small town of Lockerbie, Scotland, setting the entire village ablaze. Since I was a mature agent and spoke German, my assignment, along with many of my colleagues, was to work the cataclysmic flight.

The NTSB (National Transportation Safety Board) was formed in the mid-1960's and legitimized as a federal government agency by former President Bill Clinton. Its primary function is to coordinate guidelines and directives to federal sub-agencies when aviation disasters occur. The American Red Cross, the Department of State, the Department of Justice, the Federal Aviation Administration and the FBI are just a few of the agencies that are under the NTSB umbrella. They conversely disseminate information statewide and locally and implement a course of action in support of the airline and its disaster victims and families.

A local base of operation must be created consisting of state and local emergency response and crisis teams. The airline is responsible for notifying the next of kin, provide lodging, transportation, meals, clergy, medical doctors, emotional and logistics support at the crash site and at points of departure and arrival, in this case, JFK Airport. The Department of State is responsible for coordinating interaction with foreign embassies when disasters occur outside of the U.S.

Sequentially, official airline disaster mode tasks were assigned to executives and staff, and the course of action began.

Since Flight 103 was due that evening, securing privacy for the family members and protecting them from the media was paramount. On the Arrivals Board, in lieu of the standard ETA (estimated time of arrival) for Flight 103, the signage read, 'See Agents at Areas C and D.' Certain agents were posted there and had the task of escorting families to the First-Class lounge. Together, they walked silently through the terminal to avoid subjecting families to public scrutiny. The agents were not permitted to disclose any details and were advised only to say that information was forthcoming once they arrived at the lounge, which by then had been roped off and designated a High-Security area. The lounge, along with other JFK offices, was transformed into the official Emergency Operations Center to facilitate the necessary services.

Within the hour, local hotels purveyed catering by setting up tables around the perimeter of the lounge supplying non-stop food and alcohol. Phones with toll-free numbers were placed on tables throughout the lounge enabling families to make calls worldwide. Everyone who was assigned to work 103 assembled in the lounge and was given specific tasks. My colleagues and I were designated 'Contact' people" … front line. As Areas C and D agents escorted families into the lounge one at a time, we immediately had to verify the victim's identity via the flight manifest that we each had on a clipboard. It listed the names of all 270 passengers and crew onboard Flight 103. When we asked the family to disclose the name of the passenger they were meeting, we were required to secure vital information such as their relationship to the victim and their contact numbers. Maintaining a modem of decorum was a priority. Not having been professionally or psychologically trained in working disasters of such magnitude, inner strength and numbness enabled me to carry out my duties without falling apart emotionally as I stoically confirmed their worst nightmare: **PAN AM Flight 103 had crashed.**

All the families that I personally received at the door were my responsibility for the duration of the disaster. As it was not immediately deemed an act of terrorism, details provided to us by management trickled in and were sketchy at best. The priority at that point was for PAN AM to reconcile the flight manifest via 103's boarding passes that were lifted at the departure gate at Heathrow Airport, along with the check-in list and the final gate-check. An error in disseminating the manifest would have been as devastating as the crash itself. It was also imperative that any information we received had to be confirmed and disclosed as it came in that night from Lockerbie via London and Washington, D.C.

PAN AM's annual Christmas party was being hosted that night at one of the JFK hotels. In the airline industry, socializing at times began after 10:00 p.m. due to airline and staff scheduling. Being unaware of the crisis that awaited the world and myself, I welcomed the opportunity to temporarily allow my heart to digress from the emotional grief that I was experiencing in my personal life.

Lara, my daughter and wonderful traveling companion who was 15 yrs. old at the time, was my date for the party. She had been enroute to the airport from Long Island, New York via a car service and had no knowledge of her impending anguish. We confirmed everything the night before since she had been staying with her father during the Christmas vacation. The car would drop her off at the terminal and she was to meet me at my usual departure gate at 6:00 p.m. After my shift, we planned to first have dinner, then go home and partake in the girly-girl ritual of party prepping. In the blink of an eye, this monumental tragedy changed everything. From one of the manager's offices, I called her father's house to divert the car from coming to JFK, but she had already left, and cell phones back then were non-existent.

At approximately 5:30 p.m., the relentless and despicable pursuit for media sensationalism had already begun both in front of and inside the terminal. Hundreds of reporters swarmed in like vultures ready to attack innocent prey. They tried to force their way beyond the sealed-off ropes to gain access to the First-Class lounge. They pushed their way through barricades that protected the escorted families during their terrifying walk from Areas C and D towards the lounge where catastrophic realities awaited them.

Since clearance had already been arranged for Lara, my colleagues at the gate called me when she arrived and one of the agents escorted her up towards the lounge.

Twenty minutes later, most upset, she called me from a phone booth just outside the roped-off area. Not having any details about the crash, and as she approached, the media bombarded her with questions thinking that she had come to meet a passenger from 103. Her only refuge was to secure herself in the phone booth adjacent to the lounge until I came out and got her. In doing so, I too waded through the mass of insensitivity and insolence, pushed the cameras and microphones out of our faces and together we walked back inside.

The emotional journey that befell Lara, my colleagues and I was unsparing. The emotional journey that befell the victim's families was horrifying.

Ten feet from the lounge doors, Lara and I witnessed an agent escorting a woman who had just been traumatized by the recent death of a family member. Another family member was onboard 103. The reporters attempted to 'get the scoop' by prematurely asking her what she knew about the crash, but until then, she *hadn't* known *anything*! The curdling scream and the thud as she hit the floor remain ingrained in our hearts today as clear as the moment it happened. Spotlighted and lying unconscious on the floor, the cameras kept rolling and the reporters kept probing. Her torment was front-page news worldwide. Even after the woman collapsed, the reporters continued questioning her from the ground.

Once back inside I briefed Lara, positioned her at a table and then returned to my post at the front door while intermittently checking on her.

The ambiance in the lounge had increasingly escalated to a daunting surrealism. Watching in disbelief, Lara knew she needed to help in whatever capacity she could--offering her shoulders to cry on, her hands to hold, and her heart to those destroyed.

This is still so difficult to do after all these years. A father whose son was onboard came through the doors very angrily and immediately said to me, "This better be a serious mechanical to cause such an outrageous delay." How I wished that were the case.

I humbly asked him for the name of the passenger that he and his wife were picking up. He lunged forward and pulled my uniform jacket towards him, *screaming* in pain, "DON'T YOU DARE TELL ME MY SON IS DEAD, DON'T YOU DARE!"

Under the circumstances, as an emissary for PAN AM's horrific tragedy, how could I have expected anyone to react rationally? While fighting back my own flood of tears, I calmly advised him of the crash. His wife tried to maintain her composure long enough to ask if there were any survivors and I told her it had not yet been determined. Despite the devastating news, the families desperately clung onto the hope that somehow, somewhere, their loved ones were still alive. Chaplains and doctors were readily at hand to console or medicate. Many people went into shock, while others simply fainted in our arms. Many fell to their knees and wept uncontrollably as we cradled them like babies.

The local PAN AM VIPs started converging in the lounge to disseminate details to us from Lockerbie. We were advised that at 8:00 p.m., the CEO would come in and hold a private conference to update families, which would be followed by a national press conference outside of the lounge doors. When the CEO arrived, he entered the lounge and stood on a makeshift podium. The collective sounds of everyone's heartbeat were deafening. All terrified eyes in that room faced him, and all our arms were tightly interlocked with one another as everyone braced themselves for the unimaginable. And then, he made the official devastating announcement: "There were *NO* survivors." For the second time that night, emotional paralysis plagued the families, and their unbearable pain could be heard around the world. We all held onto them, for had we let go they would have fallen to the ground.

Hours prior to the crash, my personal pain pierced my heart with every breath I took. However, the agony around me that evening engendered a soulful epiphany and a self-analytical reality check...i.e., the love of my life was standing right next to me. She was alive and well-- I could touch her, hold her, hug her. It was then that my pain took on a new dimension, for I cried *with* Lara that night, not *for* her, unlike all those traumatized people in that room who brutally just lost *their* Laras. The slightest glimmer of hope for survival had been shattered. We stayed with our families indefinitely that night. PAN AM made arrangements for them to fly to Lockerbie the next morning on a special charter.

To this day, one of the most amazing shows of strength that Lara and I had ever witnessed was that of a loving African American family who was among my group from the onset. To help console them and all the other people, I shared my personal secular beliefs that a higher power had a greater agenda for all those beloved victims and that our destined path in life had unrelenting hurdles, and this by far, was their greatest! The woman who had lost her husband asked us all to sit in a circle and hold hands as she led us in prayer. This compassionate family comforted everyone despite their own torment. Their impenetrable faith gave them the courage to accept the reality bestowed upon them that night. Lara and I were so captivated by that incredible family. We prayed and cried with them as they reached out with genuine love to everyone in that room.

I was asked by one of the VIPs to fly to Lockerbie with my families on the 6:00 a.m. charter. My decision was instantaneous. I respectfully declined. As much as I bonded with everyone, my need to be with my child was overwhelming and she too needed me, for Lara and I shared a historical disaster that cut deep into our own reservoir of raw emotions. Around midnight our families were escorted to JFK hotels. My thoughts were... how do we say goodbye? Would we have the courage to tell them to be strong, knowing full well that their journey to *hell* would intensify within a few hours and persist for the rest of their lives?

After unending paperwork, everyone who worked the room that night desperately needed to be with one another to try and comprehend the events that had just taken place. We wondered in disbelief about the families in Lockerbie, Scotland, who were innocently wrapping Christmas presents earlier that evening. Life was simple for this sleepy little village until the night the plane fell out of the sky.

That year, the U.S. had its share of clandestine tragedies as well as in other countries that were deemed acts of terrorism. While working the room that night, I along with some of my colleagues had been informed by upper management that 103 was presumably brought down by a bomb. It was also established that night that PAN

AM officials and Washington D.C. were aware of this time-framed bomb threat since American embassies in Europe were put on alert weeks prior.

As the investigative events unfolded from month to month and year to year, even to this day, some of the truths remain elusive. Originally, the bomb was to detonate over the Atlantic Ocean. The reason for that was if it exploded over the ocean there would be no evidence or lack of it! However, the bomb itself malfunctioned. Those innocent passengers did not know that they had only 38 minutes of life remaining once *'Clipper Maid of the Seas'* lifted off the runway at Heathrow and headed north towards Scotland. So too, pertaining to the lack of relevant information, we remain notably unsettled with justifiable indignation because the bureaucratic secrecy of Flight 103 had been shrouded for a long time at the expense of our own security here in the United States.

December 21, 1988, was the day the lounge was transformed from an opulent inner sanctum for the privileged First-Class passenger to an urbane chamber of horrors for the next of Kin.

March 1989 – We now move on to the next six chapters with LTU International Airways.

Chapter 4
Dildo Dilemma

And yes, you heard/read correctly. The average flight day's success was usually determined by an on-time arrival and departure. Staff went to great lengths to turn the aircraft around in the allotted ground time, which is regulated by air traffic control, not the airline per se, as many people think. Aircrafts have designated slot times and are pushed back to hardstands, which are remote parking spaces out on the tarmac if a gate is not assigned by air traffic control or if an aircraft exceeds its gated slot time. This is a no-win situation for everyone involved.

Unbeknownst to the public, aircrafts in general are airborne most of the time. Once they arrive at a gate and the engines are shut off, the clock starts ticking and every second literally counts. The standard turnaround time for international flights is two hours and as a result, any delays in landings or departures cause a domino effect worldwide, not just locally. Each flight had its physical and mental challenges necessitating endurance and hours of after-flight paperwork.

One hot summer evening, everything was moving along at its usual intensified pace. With only ten minutes to spare before our 5:00 p.m. departure, all 408 passengers were safely buckled in their seats.

While our handling agents were securing the cargo doors, and as I made my last run up into the cockpit, one of the baggage handlers raced up to advise the captain and I that they had started offloading a bag from the cargo hold. We asked why and what was the problem. We did not want to take a delay. The handling agents heard a buzzing noise coming from a suitcase just eight minutes prior to pushback. This was bad news. An apparent delay became inevitable as our primary concerns, of course, were the safety and security of our passengers. A bit perturbed to say the least, the captain and I went down to the tarmac and waited rampside for Port Authority police while the buzzing bag was offloaded. Once it was retrieved, I took the bag-tag off and sprinted back up the stairs into the cabin. I made an announcement asking that the person whose bag-tag matched the one that I was holding up needed to identify themselves and accompany me down to the tarmac.

After a few seconds, nobody stood up. I made the announcement again but this time a bit sterner. Everyone started looking around to see who the culprit was that held up their flight.

After a minute or so, all eyes were on this elegantly dressed, perfectly quaffed middle-aged woman. She calmly stood up, never made eye contact and followed me down the stairs. Security procedures mandated that the woman open her bag in front of Port Authority police. Now mind you, all the onboard passengers that had starboard window seats (right side of the aircraft) were in full view of this tarmac tryst and it was entertaining them.

The passenger was most defiant and refused to cooperate. After advising her of the legal ramifications and the prospect of my not letting her back on the aircraft, she reluctantly opened it. And there it was… the awkward accidental activation of her colossal vibrator. It was fully encased in a black velvet bag, gold tassels and all, quite nice actually, and humming along at some serious RPMs. Holding up the departure because of a dildo debacle certainly had its repercussions.

So in lieu of an apology from this horny little half-wit, I felt that her humiliation was abundantly sufficient especially when she was told to remove the batteries in plain sight of everyone and hand them over to us. From sheer embarrassment, I'm sure she would have preferred to fly in the cargo hold all the way to Germany rather than going back up the stairs and making that walk of shame to her seat.

The distressed damsel's dildo dilemma certainly had been humiliating for her, and for me, it was exasperating because of the unnecessary involvement of Port Authority police and the waste of everyone's time. Subsequently, her bag minus the batteries was put back in the cargo hold; the cargo doors were shut, the captain gave us the thumbs up, the chocks were removed from the wheels and off they went. However, we took a useless seventeen-minute delay.

Back in my office, I had to think of the appropriate terminology for the mandatory Incident Report for Germany explaining this delay. Any delay after our 5:00 p.m. departure had to be accounted for, be it two minutes, twenty minutes or two hours. I contemplated as to what should be written and finally decided, how about Distressed Dildo Delay? Would that suffice and be politically correct?

I laughed and thought to myself, what a dummy! Was bringing it to Germany imperative, batteries and all or had she anticipated a dildo emergency upon landing? Who knew?

Afterwards down in Operations, we all took bets on the actual size of this device and concluded…ten inches. *OUCH!* We then said goodnight to each other and see you tomorrow. It was all in a day's work and just another bizarre little tale from the tarmac.

The moral of this story: follow airline regulations and remove batteries, when necessary, especially for self-pleasing tools! For happy travels, first do your homework so your journey will be delightful in every way!

Chapter 5
Pocket Money

I've often felt that intellect and intelligence are sometimes misconstrued for wisdom and common sense. One would think a prominent doctor knows that a passport is mandatory when traveling abroad.

I was called to the check-in area by our agent who advised me that Doctor & Mrs. whatever were checking in and that the good doctor left his passport at home. He argued with the agent and vehemently insisted that his New York state driver's license would suffice as proof of U.S. citizenship. It does not! The agent politely explained that she couldn't issue him a boarding pass without a passport and specifically pointed to the required documentation that was clearly printed on his LTU ticket. His immediate thought was to intimidate her into submission by publicly discrediting her competence. When the seasoned agent wasn't fazed by his egregious tantrums, he insisted on speaking with a supervisor. Knowing the problem before approaching the counter, I thought perhaps reversed psychology would help.

I introduced myself and gave him the courtesy of speaking first. After listening to his ludicrous soliloquy, I smiled and said, "Dr. whatever, surely an intelligent and worldly traveler such as yourself knows that a passport is mandatory for travel outside of the U.S." In reality, I wanted to say, you dumb schmuck, you left it home, get over it, goodbye!" However, he would not accept my dose of directives and demanded to speak with a **MAN**. Thinking he could bully me into rescinding my decision, I calmly radioed Adrian to come to the check-in area since the good doctor wanted to speak to someone with male genitalia and I just didn't have any. Adrian and I were very much in tune with one another, and he knew precisely how to intervene. As he approached, I excused myself and let him take over. The doctor told him angrily that we refused to give him his rightful boarding pass. He then took it up a couple of notches when Adrian validated the mandatory passport requirement.

Adrian then asked if he would like to speak to the Station Manager. The doctor exclaimed, "Yes, well, finally, it's about time... at least it's someone with authority, so let me talk to him." After a minute or so---surprise, surprise, guess who reappeared? Realizing he was defeated, he took me by my elbow and led me a few feet away from his wife. He secretly opened his wallet and folded several hundred-dollar bills in the palm of my hand. I regaled with delight in telling him that no amount of money would get him on our aircraft. Of course, I quickly looked down to see just how much money there was: five one-hundred dollars. Then he rudely said, "Ok *honey*, name your price within reason." Now, that angered me. Even though valuable time was being wasted, his arrogance was exasperating, so it was time to get out the big guns.

Inwardly grinning and very quietly, I told him he needed to walk over to the IAT (International Arrivals Terminal). And even though

33

it will be very busy, he must look for the Immigration officer, who is extremely tall, approximately six ft. eight in., and he will have the biggest gold badge because he's the senior officer. When you find him, tell him you are a doctor and that you are flying out on LTU this afternoon. If he gives you clearance to fly without a passport, come on back, and you're good to go. It was tough keeping a straight face while I watched him drool with delight as he left the building.

His wife stayed with their luggage while he went on his fool's errand. After only fifteen minutes, he returned and I thought to myself, oh, this should be good because it takes more than fifteen minutes to even walk over there. The good doctor advised me that the tall officer said, "No problem, of course you can go! All you must do is to have someone FedEx the passport to an address in Germany for re-entry into the U.S." Now, could that be arranged under certain extenuating circumstances? Yes, it is complicated and can be done but certainly not for such a liar. I had enough of his crap, called his bluff and insisted that we both walk back over to the IAT officer who authorized his travel. Magically, his acrimonious demeanor changed when he realized that his blatant lie didn't fly and neither would he.

I also advised him that while he went for his pretend approval, I cancelled his reservations with our airline and that he would not be accepted on any of our future flights. His wife was clearly embarrassed by his infantile behavior and his tantrums. After humbly apologizing to me, she glared at him with contempt. There were no smoochy farewells or hugs and kisses as she walked away and proceeded up to the departure gate, leaving *Pinocchio* behind.

As he stood there like a total jackass and speechless in disbelief of what had just transpired, it was my turn to take him by his elbow as he did earlier to mine and escort him to the door. I did take pleasure in telling this fool that his *pocket money* nor his title overrode common sense or the law and to have a nice day, followed by the classic airline salutation…***mmmbye bye now!***

Chapter 6
Never Neverland

When I beneath the cold red earth am sleeping and life has closed its door, will there be for me any eye weeping, that I am no more?

(SOP) Standard operating procedure for our inbound flights from Germany entailed my meeting the aircraft upon arrival on the jetway and going onboard before the passengers deplaned. The purser (chief flight attendant) and the captain would brief me of any incidents that might have occurred in-flight. As unique as some situations were, crews were always well-trained in handling airborne problems.

On this particular Sunday afternoon when the aircraft arrived at the gate and as soon as the captain turned off the engines, the purser immediately opened the forward cabin door. She was ashen in color, and the expression on her face was ghastly. I had known her for many years and as a seasoned crew member, she had a charming disposition and always handled unexpected surprises with dignity. Her first words to me were, "Oh my God, Oh my God, this was eight hours of pure hell." While walking towards her, a repugnant odor hit me like a ton of bricks, as though everyone's barf bag was filled to the max. My unsolicited reaction was *Holy Crap*, to which she emphatically replied *"Precisely,"* as she handed me the in-flight Incident Report. She along with the other crew members verbally gave me their individual accounts of the events that had transpired enroute to JFK airport.

Three hours into the flight, a passenger was heard crying from the rear of the cabin. When one of the f/a's (flight attendants) walked towards the commotion, she was overwhelmed by a horrific odor that emanated from the back. A woman had urinated and defecated in her seat and subsequently continued to do so for the duration of the flight. The passengers that were sitting near her were physically repulsed and in a timely manner, one by one they began vomiting due to the intolerable stench that permeated the area. Opening windows was certainly not an option! The crew sprayed special deodorizers posthaste that temporarily masked the offensive air which circulated throughout the fuselage.

The load factor on that trans-Atlantic flight was 360 passengers in lieu of the usual 408. Having 48 extra seats, the f/a's scrambled to relocate everyone who sat in the rear. They closed off a section by blocking as many rows as possible, along with one of the aft cabin bathrooms to keep the incident isolated. While that was being done, two other f/a's discreetly tried to take her into the toilet to remove her soiled clothing, wash her up and dress her in clean clothes that they voluntarily took out of their own personal carry-on luggage. According to the purser, when they gently tried to lift her out of her seat, she began sobbing--analogous to a small child clenching to her mother's arms in fear of being hurt or taken away. Unable to move her, the crew placed blankets around her lap and on the floor to absorb the urine and to keep it from flowing under nearby seats or down the aisles when the aircraft banked. They displayed extraordinary compassion and went far beyond the call of duty.

After observing the passenger for a while, the purser determined that she was incoherent and had no comprehension of her surroundings nor did she seem capable of speaking any languages per se. Pitiful tears just flowed from her hollow eyes as she grunted while tightly clutching her armrests. At first, given the extenuating circumstances, the captain decided to turn around and head back to Germany even though they had been airborne for almost three hours over the Atlantic Ocean. However, after a quick briefing with the crew, they all agreed to proceed to JFK since the woman was not disruptive nor were the passengers in any imminent danger.

Under normal circumstances, each f/a is assigned to work a section of the aircraft. The crew took it upon themselves to take turns working the isolated rear where she sat pathetically alone in her own feces and body fluids while perpetually rocking back and forth. As grueling as it was, the crew had to constantly placate the other passengers since they were sickened by the situation at hand. Despite the putrid stench, two in-flight meals and beverage services still had to be conducted in a congenial manner as possible. They had to serve, scour and smile.

One of the f/a's told me the story of how her swimming prowess enabled her to hold her breath long enough to quickly throw the soiled blankets in a plastic bag that were wrapped around the woman, replace them with clean ones and place a pre-cut hot lunch on the woman's tray table. When all was done, she raced into one of the bathrooms, gasped for air and feverishly scrubbed her hands. After the poor soul devoured her lunch, another f/a went to the off-limits section and removed her lunch tray. That same f/a wiped her dirty hands and face with a hot towel and for the first time eye contact was made. They exchanged a warm smile as though she finally understood that no one was going to hurt her, at least not at 38,000 feet high. Having gained a level of trust, the f/a took it a step further. She retrieved the woman's bag from the overhead bin, looked for her passport and pro-actively filled out the mandatory Immigration form that was given to passengers in-flight prior to landing. They are required for entry by Immigration.

Upon the aircraft's final approach into JFK and despite the horrendous ordeal most of the passengers had to endure for so many hours, the crew was astonished by everyone's overall compassion. Some passengers were of course incensed that the airline would allow such a 'disturbed' individual on the flight and understandably so. However, they realized that nothing could have been done, and the crew was commended for their outstanding professionalism even though barf bags became facial attachments for several of the passengers throughout the encapsulated airborne ordeal.

We all know how it gets after sitting on an aircraft during long-range flights. Upon landing, it's a mad dash towards the exit doors to get off as expeditiously as possible. After standing in the forward cabin for only a few minutes for the briefing, I couldn't fathom being trapped like that without any form of relief for over eight hours. Most of the passengers remained civil while deplaning, and in typical German fashion, they waited their turn to exit the aisles. However, it was indeed a regimented race to get out.

The f/a whom she trusted stood in the aft cabin near the rear galley. Verbally and via hand gestures, she told the reticent woman to remain in her seat, which is the SOP for handicapped passengers. I called for a wheelchair knowing she would be escorted straight through to the Arrivals Terminal. With only a few passengers left to deplane, the crew and I braced ourselves for the abhorrent task of bringing her from the rear of the cabin to the front and into the wheelchair without any further episodes. Despite the smell and her appearance, somehow the woman walked off and followed the crowd to Immigration.

Her documentation was obviously in order otherwise I would have been called by an INS officer. We assumed that given the nature of the woman's mental limitations, she'd be met at the airport by family and then… case closed! After I deplaned to continue my duties, I wondered what emotions had been stirred up by everyone and questioned my personal reaction had I been subjected to such a horrific situation. I thought eventually that the crazy lady would just be the topic of conversation and the mundane lives of all the passengers onboard that flight would recommence.

During turnarounds, there were many reasons which generated potential delays and that surely was one. Her seat had to be replaced, and the cabin had to be fumigated. The aircraft could not leave the gate for the flight back to Germany until it was deemed completely airworthy by the outbound captain. Fortunately, Delta Airlines, our contracted ground maintenance handler at that time successfully installed a new seat within the allotted ground time while Triangle Aviation Services cleaned the cabin to the best of its ability. The remainder of the afternoon's outbound operations went rather smoothly.

For all intended purposes, I was home free when those melodious words '*off the blocks*' were announced from the tarmac, i.e., the actual time of departure when the wooden chocks under the aircraft wheels were removed. In situations when aircrafts take a delay on the taxiway enroute to the runway due to congestion or inclement weather, it is not the responsibility of the airline's ground staff per se. However, this unpalatable situation was atypical and thanks to our vendors, they were successfully able to avert a departure delay at the gate despite the earlier internal condition of the fuselage.

After the departure I thought all went operationally well in Claudia's world so far that day. I contently meandered back to my office and began the tedious after-flight paperwork. The heels immediately came off my aching feet from all the running around. To unwind before beginning, I went down the hall barefoot to the

KLM lounge for a glass of wine, good Dutch cheese, a few laughs and the daily gossip with the KLM staff. Feeling all warm and fuzzy and in a skippy-day mood, I returned to the office and settled down with pen in hand. At 7:00 p.m., my happy hour ended abruptly.

I received a call from Customs that an LTU passenger had been wandering around aimlessly and since she was technically still the airline's responsibility, someone had to come and get her. My complacency instantly turned into adversity. It was apparent that no one came to the airport to meet this poor soul.

Where the in-flight crew's responsibility ended, mine had just begun and going home at a reasonable hour became a figment of my imagination. My assistant Adrian offered to walk over to IAT to get her. He radioed me on the way back and said I needed to brace myself for a monumentally unique challenge. At first, I thought he was joking. He brought the passenger to the departure terminal which by then was empty, in lieu of bringing her to our office. He told me to take deep breaths and to wrap my uniform scarf around my mouth and nose just before I approached her. This time, Adrian was not joking! I was shocked when I saw this fragile, 34-year-old tiny woman. She had porcelain skin, short brown pixie hair, and was wearing an old tee shirt with denim overalls and flip-flops on her dirty little feet. The stench that emanated from her was disgusting. She was meek, sweet-tempered and had a benevolent smile.

I asked her questions in German but soon realized she was mentally inept and could not speak. Her only sounds were grunts and cries as she vacillated between both. Adrian was told by the Customs agent that she had no luggage other than the small kiddie backpack that I gingerly removed from her shoulders. It contained an old plastic wallet with the equivalent of only ten dollars in Romanian money, one hooded sweatshirt, one tee shirt, a small comb and a new Romanian passport used for the first time for passage from Bucharest via Dusseldorf to JFK, but no return ticket back home. In that dirty old velcro wallet was the clue to her well-planned disposal; a newspaper clipping from 1971 about the opening of Disneyworld in Orlando, Florida. It was barely legible and yellowed because of its actual print age, some twenty-plus years prior. It fell apart in my hands as I tried to read it. Her hollow brown eyes lit up like a child's on Christmas morning as she grinned uncontrollably from ear to ear. Both Adrian and I were emotionally sickened and fought back our tears. Bursting with joy, she uttered the words *"Florida, Florida, Disney, Disney."* It was then that we understood why she was standing in front of us. This poor woman had been forsaken by her caretakers and deserted under the guise of visiting Disneyworld.

It was incomprehensible to us that fellow human beings were capable of discarding life as they would an old shoe or when functionality simply ceased. Had society become so jaded with the myriads of murders, wars, racism and apathy that turning the other cheek became the better part of valor? I refused to believe that people could do something so diabolical, yet there she stood with such sweet innocence as she pointed to the faded article with infantile exhilaration. It just broke our hearts because we knew her dream would never become a reality. Adrian had located a Romanian-speaking agent hoping the woman would respond in her native language, but she didn't. He stayed with her while I went back to the office to carefully read the purser's in-flight Incident Report again.

I called our Flight Operations in Germany which was manned 24/7. They checked her reservations and found a comment in her booking which stated that the passenger required onboard assistance to restrooms due to a slight mental disability. Written comments are made by a reservation/check-in agent if there are any specific requests or discrepancies noted during the check-in process. Ops (Operations) contacted the agent at the airport who checked her in earlier that morning for the westbound flight to JFK. The initials of the agent were in the passenger's computerized transaction. This is SOP with every airline should there be any repercussions… case in point. Ops was able to ascertain the details as to how this all originally manifested. Because of the seriousness and the legalities involved, an immediate investigation began. The Ops agent and I communicated back and forth all night to determine just where and when the system's and the passenger's breakdown began.

I had a far more exacerbating dilemma… what to do with her! My priority was to scrounge up some clean clothes because the smell of several loads of dried poop and urine made us all gag. I went to the lost and found office, and they offered to look for any unclaimed clothing that was available. I then called the Port Authority police and hoped that friends whom I knew were on duty. That not being the case on a late Sunday night, I presented my plight anyway and their suggestion was that they would fill out reports and bring her to a hospital for psychological evaluation. I felt she didn't stand a chance in hell of surviving and graciously declined. Just then, one of the kind KLM agents came into my office with a pair of old pajama pants and tee shirt that she found in an unclaimed suitcase. I was ecstatic and planted a big kiss on her forehead. Adrian managed to keep her perched on a bench by giving her firm yet non-threatening directives analogous to a dog's commands such as-- sit, stay.

Adrian handled some of my reports for me that night while I figured out what to do next. At 9:00 p.m. I sent him home since there wasn't much more he could do. Then a sickening task awaited me since her appearance and odor were unbearable. I took her to the ladies' room and handed her the old pants and shirt. After gentle coaxing, she timidly removed her soiled overalls. I pointed to the garbage can and then to her underwear that was fused to her raw, blistered skin. Reluctantly, she took them off. I attempted to wash only her hands and face, but she started crying and backed away. I mimicked washing, and she slowly came over and put her hands in the sink, never taking her eyes off me. In my estimation, she had been a feral child. My thoughts ran amok as I mentally recapped my contractual LTU employment agreement; coercing a mentally ill woman to disrobe in an airport bathroom was *not* in my job description! It was all so debasing. Enrage and self-pity had taken over, yet I repeatedly kept telling myself she's a human being, don't throw her away along with the feces-infested clothes and treat her with kindness.

After regaining my composure, I handed her paper towels. My compassion must have momentarily registered in her disconnected world because with a faint smile she reached out to touch my hand, and while awkwardly drying herself off she displayed a level of trust.

After the bathroom breakthrough, I took her hand, and we walked upstairs to Pizza Hut which was in the process of closing. Fortunately, the guys knew me, and they heated up two pizzas. She was ravenous and ate like an animal and as expected, she was totally devoid of any table etiquette. Her only sounds were happy grunts.

We then walked over to IAT to speak with the Traveler's Aid Society to see if they could provide shelter for one night while I secured passage back to Romania for her on a flight the next morning. The agent saw that I was in dire need of their services. She advised me that she could only provide one-way bus fare to New York City to go to the consulate and one meal voucher at a JFK eatery. Now I ask you…what good would that have done me, especially on a Sunday night? She displayed apathy, not empathy! That was the extent of her 'aid.' For a job such as that, compassion is a prerequisite. She seemed to have been inconvenienced by my desperate attempts for help, however her isolated attitude was not the norm since the Traveler's Aid Society had always been a blessing to stranded passengers. As exhausted and angry as I was with a zero-batting average, I refused to acquiesce. We walked all the way back to the departure hall where I once again perched her on 'the bench.' Despite my mounting frustrations, discarding this poor soul was not an option. I had the luxury of going home, eventually. I was loved. I was rational nor was I ever abandoned. After all, she was a human being. We were kindred sisters.

Feeling defeated and up against a brick wall, I called acquaintances who managed a JFK hotel and advised them of my downhill plight. They immediately helped and said they would meet us in the lobby. By then, it was 11:00 p.m. when we arrived at the hotel via auto-link. Like happy little people, we all got into the elevator and proceeded to the room that the managers set aside for her. I turned down her bed and once again took her into the bathroom and mimicked washing. We all made sure that she saw the security guard who was positioned outside of her door until the morning. Before leaving her room, I pointed to the clock and held up seven fingers hoping she grasped what I meant and hoped that she understood I'd be back for her at 7:00 a.m. in the morning. She grunted and grinned; we smiled and left.

Any costs incurred for unforeseen services, such as hotels, meals, transport etc., are generally paid for by the carrier based on the airline manager's discretion. My hotel friends also planned to have breakfast sent to her room at 7:00 a.m. on Monday morning, at which time I was going to pick her up. After many grueling hours of drama and on the way back from the hotel to my office, I breathed a sigh of relief knowing that she was safe at least for that night.

Since LTU did not operate Monday flights, I called a manager friend at Lufthansa Airlines and explained the circumstances to her. Without hesitation, she made the necessary arrangements for a flight the next day and buffered the aft cabin. Airlines in general have unwritten codes of reciprocity with one another. They are most helpful in re-accommodating passengers. Airports become your second home and employees become family. When a crisis occurs, they rally together and become a part of the solution. Assuming that the woman was sound asleep under guarded supervision, I finally headed home at 1:00 a.m. In order of priority, I took off my uniform, threw it in the outside garbage bin, took a hot shower and wrapped myself in flannel pajamas. LTU provided staff with two complete uniforms and all the accessories, which were in my closet. Since I was starving and too tired to make anything to eat, a box of chocolate chip cookies and milk hit the spot.

Shortly after a few minutes of channel surfing to unwind, I exploded into sleep only to be viciously awakened at 3:30 a.m. by a call from the hotel manager frantically advising me that the woman was *gone*! Somehow, she walked out of the room unnoticed. Prior to calling me, a search of the entire hotel and the outside grounds had already been made. According to the *'INSECURITY'* guard who was assigned the simple task of securing her room, he had repeatedly knocked on her door at approximately 2:30 a.m. When there was no answer, he had the front desk call her room, at which point they notified the managers who lived on-site. Realizing he obviously left his post or that he slept on the job wasn't exactly rocket science, for it begged the questions…why did he knock on her door at 2:30 a.m. and how did this happen? None of it made any sense. There wasn't anything deviant about the woman, therefore I was positive she did not maliciously sneak out. When the managers opened the door, the bed had not even been slept in nor were any of the bathroom amenities used other than the bar of soap I opened when we first got to her room.

I was just devastated that in the middle of the night, in a questionable JFK neighborhood, this damaged child walked into oblivion. Physically and emotionally, I was on overload and told myself that from a humanitarian perspective I did everything possible short of having her committed. For me, it was not a feasible option and yet in my heart I felt responsible for her disappearance. I castigated myself with the proverbial should-haves. I then called the Port Authority police again and they put out an alert hoping she'd be found roaming the streets. We also called the local police precincts and hospitals. However, that was an exercise in futility.

In the interim, our Ops in Germany had contacted the check-in agent and the crew of the inbound flight that day. The following was determined: the check-in agent clearly remembered that the passenger was accompanied by another woman of similar stature and age. When the two were on the LTU queue in Germany, they approached the counter together with proper documentation. The older woman did all the talking while the other woman just quietly stood behind her. A seat was requested in the aft cabin stating that her 'sister' was a bit slow and required privacy and occasional bathroom assistance. FYI…in-flight crews are not responsible for passenger bathroom assistance unless a dire emergency occurs while airborne. The agent hesitated for a moment but felt there wasn't anything inappropriate, so she accommodated the request and noted it on the computer.

However, she did make a wise decision before issuing her the boarding pass. She excused herself and went into the Ops office directly behind her which was visible from the counter. There, she approached the captain who was to operate the flight to New York. He was in the process of his pre-flight briefing. She asked him to go look at the passenger and assess her ability to fly since the agent was skeptical about her appearance. The captain peered from the Ops office as the agent pointed her out. He observed her from afar and felt she was not a threat to the other passengers. They both agreed that more comments should be entered into her record locator. The agent then issued the boarding pass and both women proceeded to the departure gate. Prior to 9/11, passengers were allowed to be accompanied to the departure gate by family etc. Since no dialogue was necessary for boarding, the older woman asked the gate agents if she could escort her sister to the aircraft door and was given permission to do so. Then, one of the f/a's took the woman to her seat. Just before the aircraft doors closed, the crew was given the usual load-sheet, which is a printout of weight and balance and all operational information pertinent to the flight per se, inclusive of this passenger's check-in comments entered by the agent. That was the beginning of her end!

Based on the investigation, it was determined that a woman purchased a ticket for the passenger with new cash at a travel agency in Bucharest, Romania two days prior to the flight and paid full fare, no questions asked. That in itself was out of the norm and should have raised a red flag. According to the travel agent, the anonymous purchaser seemed nervous and in a hurry to complete the transaction. She gave a fictitious name, address and telephone number as the contact and claimed that the passenger was her sister. The travel agent also disclosed that a roundtrip ticket was indeed purchased otherwise she could not have issued just a one-way fare, which the imposter obviously knew. The return ticket back to Romania was never given to the passenger.

It was and shall always remain incomprehensible to me that a human being could be rejected in such a cruel manner because she was a burden to her caretakers. Her wretched existence was blatantly expendable. No one knew what happened to her in the streets of New York. It haunted me for years. One of my silly coping mechanisms has always been to neatly compartmentalize issues in my brain and deal with them in order of priority. It alleviates the all-too-familiar emotional overload. I tried to convince myself that she was somewhere safe. When my imaginary supposition lost internal credibility and to console myself, I remembered reading the words of Socrates just as he was about to poison himself with hemlock; *"To die and be released."* He couldn't bear the injustice of a society that falsely condemned him to life imprisonment. She too was unjustly imprisoned in a psychological hell. I had to believe that her possible demise was the lesser of all evils and that metaphysically she crossed over and went home to a kinder existence. Despite my personal 'in-depth' involvement, LTU Operations in Germany, Port Authority police, NYC police, the German police and the Romanian police departments, she was never found!

Henry Thoreau, the prolific philosopher and poet, succinctly once wrote about an Indian woman who was vilified by society. 'No one heard the beat of her drum. No one else heard her drumbeat that thumped in the farthest reaches of her awareness.' I could only have hoped that this poor soul was not cognizant of her personal depravity and that she ultimately and painlessly reached her own beloved Disneyworld!

Chapter 7
UM-Planned Parenthood

When children travel alone between the ages of seven and fourteen, they are considered UMs (unaccompanied minors). Since they are the airline's responsibility, the ground and in-flight crews follow strict guidelines in handling these precious young passengers.

During check-in at the departure terminal, a family member must fill out mandatory forms which contain pertinent information for the child's safety and security. These signed forms, along with their travel documents, are then placed in a plastic pouch issued by the agent and placed around the child's neck and must not be removed. The parent then escorts the UM to the departure gate and when boarding commences, an agent brings the child onboard to a set of rows designated for UMs and secures the child in his pre-assigned seat. Upon arrival at the final destination, the UM remains seated until the other passengers deplane. The UM is then taken off by an agent who brings him/her to Immigration, Customs and baggage claim. When all is done, the child is handed over in the Arrivals Terminal to a family member who must sign for his release. In general, it is an amiable, secure modus operandi, and children usually consider it fun.

Upon the arrival of our routine flight, an agent called my office to advise me that they had a 12-year-old UM and his luggage, but no parents to sign for him. I asked the agent to wait a half hour or so assuming that the parents might have encountered traffic. An hour later, still no parents. I then told the agent to bring the child over to me and, in addition to my usual operational responsibilities, babysitting had been added to the evening's to-do list. He was a little darling, not at all stressed and took it in stride. After a few minutes of introducing myself and making small talk, I called the UM's home, and an answering machine picked up.

I left a message saying that they needn't be worried about their son because he was safe and secure in my office. The two of us kept looking at the door as we reassured one another that the distraught parents would appear at any moment, grab their little boy in their arms, and kiss and hug him all over. An hour later, it was apparent that this Kodak moment was not happening any time soon.

Since I had to be rampside for our 5:00 p.m. outbound departure, I took a few minutes to think about the rest of the day. I told the UM to sit in my office and not to move until I returned. I also told him to answer the phone and take messages.

The most hectic Operational time for all of us was in the late afternoon and work-related calls for me came through our radios. Any calls received at my desk were only personal, and it made him feel important that he had this responsibility. Being crazy busy around 4:00 p.m., the poor little guy was still patiently sitting at the desk, so I brought him downstairs into Flight Operations when the outbound captain and the crew arrived from our New York City crew hotel to do their pre-flight briefing. He was fascinated and asked the captain to sign his logbook. I told the crew in German about the situation. The captain then told the child not to worry because mom and dad were probably on their way and that he was in good hands. I thought to myself, he is just an incredibly mature young man, or he's been there/done that before. I wasn't quite sure yet.

After our 5:00 p.m. departure, I was certain that by the time I returned from the tarmac, June and Ward Cleaver and the 'Beave' would be merrily on their way back to Connecticut singing Kumbaya. Not so. He was doodling on a piece of paper when I walked in. He then anxiously looked up and asked me if his parents had arrived. I checked again with the staff downstairs and as expected, they hadn't-- another long night of surprises for me at JFK!

Since food is the way to a young man's heart and stomach, up we went to good old Pizza Hut. I put my paperwork aside for a while so my cute little hip attachment wouldn't feel abandoned. His apprehension over the missing parents was now obvious. As we ate, I asked him all about school, sports, and what he did for the two months while visiting his grandparents in Munich…anything that was a mental diversion. By 8:30 p.m., I took his hand and assured him that we'd stay together as long as necessary even if it meant bringing him home with me for the night. I couldn't think of anything else to say to make him feel secure.

Back in my office, I had him write down phone numbers from friends, family and neighbors, but all calls were unsuccessful. Then I asked if he would like to assist me in my paperwork. He counted the tickets, ran downstairs to Operations, and actually had fun because as he said, it was a new experience for him.

My fear was that the parents had gotten into a serious accident, rendering them powerless to call. What other possible reasons were there? Only something tragic would have warranted such parental delinquency. Why hadn't anyone called? With a heavy heart and mind, I started preparing to be the potential bearer of bad news for this lovable UM.

It had been more than *six* hours with no communication from his family. How much longer could I wait before implementing a course of action? Even though we bonded, he was frightened and his anxiety became apparent. The poor little guy's voice quivered when he spoke, and his legs were jiggling uncontrollably under the desk.

Despite his adolescent macho bravado, it became difficult for him to focus. He was visibly shaken. Under the pretense of wanting sweets, I sent him to the First-Class lounge to fill his pockets with goodies. Of course, I called the lounge and they gladly accommodated him. It also gave me the opportunity to start putting a discerning game-plan into action. Just before calling Operations in Germany and beginning the unpleasant process, one final attempt was made to reach his parents.

To my pleasant surprise, his mother answered. It was a big relief. However, my patience was tested when I asked her if she received any of the messages that I left regarding her distressed son's arrival. When I discussed everything with her, I shall never forget her answer, which was-- oh, was that today? I did my best to curtail my contempt and replied, are you serious? She said they thought their son was arriving the following day due to the time change. Did she not confirm his return date and ETA? She told me she forgot about the time difference and asked me what it was. I assured her that the universal clock had not changed in the last two months while her son was in Germany.

The conversation really got stupid when the award-winning mother-of-the-year was told that she had to be at JFK within the next two hours or her son would be handed over to proper authorities. However, I had no intention of doing anything so drastic. When the UM returned with a tray of goodies, I excitedly motioned to him that his mom was on the phone. He then shed happy tears and we did a few high-fives as he hurriedly walked over to the desk. She did not ask to speak to her anguished child! And are you ready for her response? She asked if I could check him into a local hotel and she started giving me credit card information as though I was his au pair or a front desk receptionist. She promised she would pay me back. What a sport! Since her son was standing right next to me, it was really an effort to keep my composure while discreetly cursing her preposterous request.

She begrudgingly relented and said, "Well, I guess you give us no choice but to drive all the way to the airport *NOW*!" At 12:45 a.m., dumb and dumber finally showed up while the father waited curbside in the car. He didn't even come in to greet his son. The mother walked into the terminal with a surly attitude that I wanted to knock right out of her. As we approached his mom, she barely embraced her son, considering his ordeal.

Despite breathing a sigh of relief, the emotional anguish and physical exhaustion took a toll on him. As the stoic young man ran towards her, he wept, asking repeatedly, "Mom, where were you, where were you?" Unfortunately, I had to be civil and could not display my contempt in front of this innocent child. So instead, I gave him a big hug and thanked him for his help and his wonderful company.

Then I gave him my home number and told him to call me any time for any reason should he have parental issues in the future. I'd like to think the maternally inept woman understood my underlying message. I had her sign the UM release and an Incident Report that I filled out, advising her that both would remain on file indefinitely.

As I watched them exit the terminal at 1:00 a.m. for a flight that came in at 3:00 p.m., I couldn't help but think how traumatic it had to be for this sweet child and questioned the quality of his home life. That was surely a first for me and as a mother myself, it was inconceivable. There was no justification for their despicable parental negligence.

A few days later, I mailed a package to this darling boy which contained the LTU model of the aircraft type that he flew in along with the other usual LTU souvenirs: a poster, tee-shirt, keychain, pen and a mug plus my thank you note for helping me and for giving me the opportunity to spend time with such an incredible young man. That was how I wanted him to *remember* the day his parents *forgot*!

Chapter 8
Have A Drink *On* Me

Once upon a time, there was a pretty young maiden who lived on a huge farm in Lancaster, Pennsylvania. She was an only child of German immigrants who adorned their little girl with all the luxuries their hard-working hands could provide.

Now mind you, the young princess did not lift a finger to help her mom and pop. That would have been beneath her. She did not want to feel the wind in her hair nor run her manicured little fingers through the rich, fertile soil and stepping in cow poop with her Gucci shoes would have been reasons for hysteria. Despite her opulent lifestyle, at 21 years old, she had never left the comforts of the farm. When traveling interstate, her mode of transportation was the shiny sports car her parents bought her.

Aerophobia is a fear of flying. Ironically, there is a slight correlation between the character in Erica Jong's 1973 iconic novel, Fear of Flying and that of our femme fatale in this story. Both had the need for self-discovery and liberation after being emotionally sheltered for many years. Like any phobia, fear of flight can have serious repercussions if not handled properly. Aerophobics do not have a fear of the aircraft per se, but rather the actual *disconnect* from solid ground to flight. Fainting, rapid heart rate, nausea, trembling and severe sweating are just a few of the symptoms.

(*Acrophobia* is an irrational fear of heights *anywhere* that impacts daily life.)

One morning, while preparing for the day's flight, I received a phone call from a woman with a heavy German accent advising me that her daughter was a first-time flyer and that she was extremely nervous about her pending flight that afternoon.

Mom was very sweet and apologetic for having burdened me. She asked if the crew and I could provide a little TLC, given her baby girl's flying apprehensions. I told Mom to have her daughter page me upon check-in, and I would gladly try to alleviate her fears.

At 2:00 p.m., three hours prior to departure, she arrived from Lancaster, Pennsylvania, via a private car service all the way to New York. I prepared a little pep-talk for her and had already blocked two bulkhead seats so she would feel comfortable since this was her first time flying. Upon approaching the counter, I expected to see a little German chubby-cheeker or a Rebecca of Sunnybrook Farms. However, my jaw dropped when instead, Lolita of Lancaster (not her real name) greeted me with a big smile, a warm hug and a jar of mom's homemade jam. She was a stunning beauty with bouncing, behaving hair and the antithesis of what I had expected. Her clothes were to die for, as was her body because she was obviously very well pampered... no dirt under her acrylic nails! Her personality was effusive and a bit naive as she expressed giddy excitement along with a bit of demure angst.

After she checked in, I walked her upstairs to the departure level and requested a brief synopsis of her travel experiences. Well, she didn't have any! She confessed that she was petrified of flying but was determined to spread 'her wings' for the first time on 'our wings' to visit cousins in Germany. After my pep-talk, I excused myself and suggested that since she had three hours until the departure, perhaps *sipping* a glass of white wine might help her relax and that at 3:45 p.m. I would meet her back at the check-in counter to reinforce my pep-talk and be done with it.

She was very grateful, gave me more hearty hugs and off she went. An hour later, when I was meeting the inbound flight, Adrian called me on his radio asking if I could come to the counter because a passenger was extremely upset and needed to speak with me immediately. When I arrived, there was Lolita, three sheets to the wind (intoxicated, tanked, drunk, smashed) and sobbing hysterically.

I had very little time to spare but felt that since it was my initial foolish wine suggestion that got her drunk to begin with, I had to be tolerant. I asked her how many glasses of wine she had to which she replied, "oh, I didn't have any wine." I responded with, **SOOOO** what happened? Being such a beauty, the bartender happily engaged her in conversation, and she revealed her acute fear of flying. He recommended stronger moonshine to help calm her nerves. What a swell guy! Three martinis later, her fear of flying intensified.

I advised her that it would be in her best interest to offload her luggage, send her back home and reschedule for another time. She wailed at that suggestion and pleaded with me to please let her go. "Please, please, I'll sober up, I promise," she repeated in her drunken stupor. It was a tough call for me because the trip was very important to her, however, based on her inebriated condition, I just felt I couldn't let her fly. Fear, alcohol and altitude do not mix. This beauty cried, begged, slobbered all over my uniform jacket, had snot hanging from her nose, and it was all my fault. The guilt pulled at my heartstrings, and I weakened. I read her the riot act about having one hour to completely sober up or it was a no-go. She promised to get a hot meal and have strong coffee. Lolita was then a happy little girl and swore she would make me proud. Off she went again to the departure lounge, of course after many more sloppy but sincere hugs.

At 4:50 p.m., boarding had almost been completed. The agents and I were counting the boarding passes for a gate-check. I thought to myself that Lolita must have already gone onboard but wondered why she hadn't said goodbye, or had she purposely tiptoed past me so I wouldn't deny her boarding again. The count was off by one. We feverishly recounted several times and still no gate-check. I ran onboard to see if she was in her seat. She wasn't. Before deplaning, I so hoped to hear the pitter-patter of drunken Gucci feet running up the jetway, but I didn't. My thoughts were that her fear of flying along with the three martinis put her over the top, and she split, forfeiting her ticket and purposely leaving her luggage behind for pick up on another day. I had her paged several times but to no avail.

By then, it was our 5:00 p.m. departure time and after explaining to the captain why I felt this passenger was a no-show, we immediately had her bags offloaded so he could leave the gate. This procedure can be done relatively fast because the baggage handlers know in which cargo hold everyone's bags are placed.

Just then, one of the gate agents came running up the jetway and said, "she's here and good luck!" We immediately stopped the offloading of her bags via radio, and I went out to get her. Oh my God! I cringed because she was even *more* drunk than before. She staggered over to me and started crying again. And her breath-- rancid! I grabbed her by the elbow, quickly bypassed the purser who was busy in the front galley, and I sat the little drunk in her bulkhead seat. I told her to *zip it* because the captain would evaluate her condition and then his decision would be out of my hands.

After buckling her seatbelt and through clenched teeth, I strongly reiterated--keep your mouth shut, got it? Still whimpering, she promised and bobbed her head up and down. Out comes the perturbed captain from the cockpit. He had every right to be annoyed because by then we had already taken an unnecessary fifteen-minute delay. I felt responsible and told him that she was harmless and she'd fall asleep once the aircraft was airborne. He then went right over to her and asked very sternly--how much did you have to drink? With that question, the slurring Lolita became hysterical, shook

64

uncontrollably, grabbed both armrests and started yelling," we're going to die, aren't we!" Her frantic outburst was followed by projectile vomiting that landed on my shoes and on my legs since I was standing in front of her by the bulkhead.

Need I say what the captain's decision was*.....OUT !!* While the f/a's angrily cleaned the bulkhead wall from the splattered martini puke, I went into the bathroom, took off my pantyhose and washed the vomit off my legs and shoes. The baggage handlers had already been instructed to once again remove her luggage STAT. After she cleaned herself off with wet paper towels, one of the f/a's handed her a barf bag and lead us to the door. I apologized for Lolita's puking and my stupidity. The purser abruptly said, "*Aufwiedersehen!*" (goodbye) and closed the cabin door. So, there we were on the jetway heading back to the gate.

Even though I encouraged her to have only one glass of wine in lieu of downing three martinis, I made a wrong judgment call and had to face the consequences. In total, we took a 40-minute delay because of this fiasco. One of the gate agents volunteered to bring her back downstairs to the terminal.

I booked an airport hotel room and arranged for an auto-link to pick her up. My infuriated reaction when she attempted to apologize and hug me was *DO NOT* come near me! Once she was gone, I then called her parents to advise them of her medicinal martini binge and that their sleeping beauty would require transportation and a lot of mouthwash in the morning.

I smelled awfully vomity for the rest of the day and gave my poor shoes the proper burial when I got home. The repercussions for my managerial faux pas were the forty-minute flight delay, vomit legs, ruined shoes, and a jar of jam.

A few days later Lolita tracked me down to humbly apologize again. She excitedly told me that she had booked another flight for the following week and to make sure I would be there. I thought to myself, is she serious? I respectfully advised her that she wouldn't be accepted on any flights with her current aerophobia and proceeded to recommend psychological therapy, not liquid therapy. I can forgive much of anything, but puking on my shoes was a very, very bad thing to do.

She had three martinis too many and literally *ALL* on me!

Chapter 9
Midsummer Night's Dream

Before beginning our last LTU story, I would like to reiterate what hardstands and planemates are since they're relevant to our next episode. A hardstand is a remote paved parking spot for aircrafts after landing that are out on the tarmac if a gate is not provided for them by Air Traffic Control while on final approach. In lieu of a gate, Air Traffic Control assigns these designated parking spots for the aircraft. A hardstand is also assigned to an aircraft if it exceeds its gated slot time. A planemate is a hydraulic vehicle used in transporting passengers via the tarmac to and from an aircraft if a gate is not available.

I added this particular tale to exemplify the necessary sacrifices that airline staff and all public servants must make at times, and I was no exception. The following is my personal story:

If the traveling public were aware of the intricacies that are involved in flight operations, they would be more amenable to airport staff when distress situations occur. Occasionally, passengers had legitimate gripes especially when gate agents failed to disclose the basis of a delay. Not informing them simply proliferates their anxieties and it also intimates that they are morons and not worthy of truthful explanations. I had always encouraged my staff to be honest with passengers because the more they knew, the quieter they were.

An aircraft has various radar systems, one being primary radar and a secondary system called a transponder. In brief, this is an electronic device in the cockpit that transmits signals to and from Air Traffic Control in providing pressure altitude, positioning and collision avoidance within controlled airspace. There were occasions when an inbound flight would come into JFK with a mechanical problem that was identified by a captain while still airborne. When possible, arrangements and equipment required to rectify issues were made in preparation prior to the aircraft's arrival.

On one such occasion while airborne over Bangor, Maine, our inbound captain notified me and JFK Operations at 12 noon that the transponder had malfunctioned enroute and needed to be replaced within the two-hour allotted ground time. As mentioned previously in other chapters, my social life was usually in jeopardy due to the nature of the airline industry. For many years I had to work weekends and holidays. I had no choice since flights did not come in on my schedule. I accepted this, not graciously at times but nonetheless, it was a part of my job yet a bone of contention when plans were made that had to be cancelled. When receiving the transponder news from the captain, I became somewhat despondent.

That Saturday night, I had an extremely exciting once-in-a-lifetime social commitment and was determined to go no matter what. I brought evening clothes to the airport as I had done many times, only to be disappointed due to a bad flight day that totally ruined my personal plans. So there I was, faced with yet another social crisis because of a stupid transponder. I went into acute deployment mode and started organizing a fail-proof plan which I implemented immediately. Considering the avionic level of this particular challenge, I wasn't in total denial about incurring a reasonable outbound delay.

My first frantic call was to our maintenance handler at Delta Airlines. After explaining the situation to him, he checked and then advised me that they didn't have a transponder in stock. However, he was able to get one from their headquarters in Atlanta, Georgia. I told him that I needed it on the JFK tarmac in two hours and installed within one hour for our 5:00 p.m. departure. He laughed. I stressed and after snapping back to reality, I took the mature approach and started begging. He must have felt bad and put me on hold for several anxiety-prone minutes and came back with good news.

A Delta flight was leaving from Atlanta to New York at 1:45 p.m. He offered to make arrangements to get it onboard that Delta flight, as well as to have it taken off the aircraft and delivered to whomever I sent for pick up. I was so grateful and sincerely expressed my gratitude especially since Delta had always been reliable in the past. I thought ok, this was just a little too easy... there had to be a catch. Based on past mechanicals, unforeseen problems didn't always go smoothly. If a certain aircraft part was required, getting it was contingent upon availability. Fortunately, due to LTU's high aircraft maintenance level in Germany, problems were an infrequent occurrence. Getting the new transponder to New York was not without its challenges. The thrills and the '*Oh Crap*' moments had just begun.

Problem #1. The Delta flight from Atlanta was landing at LaGuardia Airport in lieu of JFK Airport. Now under any other circumstances, that wouldn't have been an issue. Without traffic the drive between both airports was approximately 45 minutes. However, on a hot summer weekend, the traffic would be dreadful. That alone became a threat for executing my plans in a timely manner. Nonetheless, it was a minor glitch and with a little nip and tuck certainly doable, I hoped.

My next critical call was to our captain who was flying the aircraft back to Germany that evening. He was at our New York City crew hotel getting ready for crew pick-up to JFK. I advised him of the situation, and he was thoroughly impressed by my proactive initiatives especially when I told him that a replacement transponder would be rampside within three hours. He asked if this was confirmed and I said *absolutely*. I then hung up and had no clue as to how I would do this or how it would play out.

Problem #2. I could not send a staff member over to LaGuardia to pick up the transponder because of the time of day that it was…our busiest, nor could I leave myself. My only recourse was to have someone pick it up. Relying on a delivery service was far too risky assuming that they may not be reliable for something so critical, in addition to getting the transponder of course, but my pending date that night as well. Nor could I trust a stranger to meet with the Delta contact at LaGuardia that was going to personally offload the transponder and hand it to whomever I sent over. No... this had to be placed in someone's hands who was completely responsible and trustworthy. I quickly went through my mental phone book and thought of the perfect person who had been dependable during our courtship a year prior.

Even though we remained friends and despite my urgent predicament, it took tenacity to call my friend Phil and ask him. I had nothing to lose and everything to gain. Had he selfishly declined to go on this radical little journey for me, my only option was to pray for divine intervention and sacrifice myself for a night or two at a local convent. Fortunately for me, Phil was home just relaxing poolside. Unfortunately for him, he lived over an hour and a half away from LaGuardia Airport and on that hot Saturday afternoon, negotiating the traffic was going to be very nasty. He wasn't exactly overjoyed but he did agree to go.

We diligently rehearsed all the coordinates. I emphasized complete with shameless blame, should he accept the assignment, the responsibility was on his shoulders to get that transponder from LaGuardia Airport and into my hands in record time. FYI, Phil was handsomely reimbursed by our airline with a generous Amex gift card and two round-trip tickets to Germany. Not too shabby, right?

Time was of the essence, and all was in place. The transponder was airborne from Atlanta enroute to LaGuardia Airport and my buddy Phil was enroute from Long Island to LaGuardia as well. The outbound crew was enroute to JFK, and Delta mechanics were on the tarmac ready with tools in hand.

At 3:00 p.m., our handling agents and I were anxiously waiting rampside for our inbound LTU flight that was taxiing to the hardstand assigned by Air Traffic Control. The passengers were then offloaded via planemates in lieu of a gate.

Before I continue, I'd like to share a little aviation history with you: Passengers are always enplaned and deplaned on the **port** side, which is the left. Ancient Mariners docked their ships at ports on the left to on/offload their crews and cargo otherwise they would have fallen into the water had they exited **starboard** side which is the right. Since planes are referred to as ships, airports have adhered to this procedure. At most airports, the jet bridges are built to accommodate planes that are aligned facing them, which is another reason why they board and disembark on the port side. Also, captains sit in the left chair in a cockpit to give them better visual parking access and it's easier for them to monitor wingtip clearances at airports that do not have jet-bridges. In addition, basic standard airport traffic patterns are left-handed.

Now that you have gained some insight into ramp protocol, back at the hardstand, one of our reputable handling agents, Triangle Aviation Services, hooked up their mobile truck-mounted stairs on the starboard side, which is standard procedure. These remote stairs are designated strictly for   access into the cabin for cleaning and catering crews. Fueling, off/onloading baggage and cargo are all starboard activities as well. For safety reasons, passengers embark/disembark only port side. I went up into the cockpit to speak with the inbound captain. He had already signed the aircraft over to Delta, who immediately began removing the faulty transponder.

In the meantime, back at the terminal, the agents were busy checking in the passengers who were unaware of my extraordinary efforts to harmoniously mitigate an on-time departure, purely for selfish reasons that day. They were happy little people, oblivious of their pending anguish or of my personal commitment to fulfill one of my once-upon-a-time dreams that night. After returning to the terminal from the tarmac at 3:30 p.m. with the aircraft in the capable hands of the Delta mechanics, I continued with my usual operational responsibilities and thought to myself that I orchestrated this avionic challenge in record time. After all, it was a social emergency.

The flight from Atlanta to LaGuardia was due to arrive at 3:45 p.m. After landing, Delta would call me, at which point I would then contact Phil on his car phone to give him the rendezvous details. The unnerving call from Delta came through on time as did my gallant liaison. Upon proudly completing his mission, he called to advise that the traffic from LaGuardia to JFK was at a total standstill, so I quickly rerouted him via local streets. The poor guy was under such pressure that he stuttered. As per our coordinated plan, he called just before he got to our terminal. I then ran out to intercept his car and jumped in. I felt awful because he was sweating and trembling as a result of his three-hour traumatic ordeal. However, without a second to spare, he handed me the new transponder. I jumped out, shut the door and abruptly said, 'Thanks, call me.' The Holy Grail was finally in my arms at 4:50 p.m. High heels and all, I sprinted over people's luggage in the terminal and guarded this heavy transponder as if it were a priceless antique.

At 5:00 p.m., our normal departure time, the handling agent and I immediately drove it out to the aircraft and gave it to Delta who began the installation. I then raced back up to the departure gate where over 300 restless passengers were anxiously waiting to board the flight that should have already left. While running, my gate agents informed me via radio that they made the appropriate delay announcement. I suggested that they do not disclose the nature of the delay nor give a new ETD (estimated time of departure) until Delta assessed the time frame: one hour was their estimated repair time, so I set a new ETD for 6:45 p.m. Logistically, that gave Delta a one-hour and forty-five-minute window. Upon approaching the passengers up at the gate, they encircled me like vultures ready to bite their prey. My immediate thought was to grab the microphone and say,' Ok, folks, just be quiet--go sit yourselves down and deal with it. At least you're all going to Germany tonight, albeit a bit later than scheduled, but my plans are going down the toilet real quick, so suck it up and get over it.' However, in lieu of that hissy fit, my calm announcement consisted of exactly what had transpired all afternoon inclusive of every precise detail so the passengers could appreciate all that the staff and I were doing to get them to Dusseldorf as soon as possible. At the podium, the usual redundant questions from the passengers began; how much longer, when are we leaving, is the aircraft ready? At 6:40 p.m., the mechanics came up to the gate and advised me that they required yet another thirty minutes. I promptly shared this upsetting update with everyone. As you can imagine, the passengers were most frustrated and rightly so.

Still trying to be optimistic that my social fairytale would come to fruition perhaps a tad later than anticipated, I requested three planemates to transport everyone to the aircraft that was out on the hardstand. Since these planemates were used by many airlines, it was important to secure their usage in advance, although we were only allowed to call approximately twenty minutes prior to needing them. When they arrived, we started loading each one as quickly as possible. Each planemate held approximately 125 passengers. All the passengers bid me an earnest and heartfelt farewell. Underneath my airline smile, my thoughts were… all right, no time for chitchat, come on folks, hurry up, let's move it.! The in-flight outbound crew that was already onboard was advised via radio that I was releasing the first planemate with the passengers, then the second, then the third. It took thirty minutes to load all three and get them out to the aircraft. When they arrived, the purser (chief flight attendant) checked with the mechanics who were still working onboard. Even though they required an additional fifteen minutes, she opened the cabin door and told our handling agents that we could release the planemates for boarding. Since the delay impinged on the crew's flight-duty time, they too were equally as anxious to head back to Germany.

Then, with everything in place, our handling agent drove me back out to the aircraft. When we got there, I was incensed that none of the planemates had been offloaded since the passengers were still onboard. With panic and nausea, I bolted up the stairs into the cockpit to find out why the crew hadn't allowed the passengers to board. The captain then calmly told me to send all passengers back to the gate *'indefinitely'* because there was yet another problem with the transponder output tube. Everything else he said thereafter became a blur and registered only as blah blah blah.

So there it was, another fiendish plot to decimate my plans for an extraordinary evening and bring it to a sadistic end. Not only was I devastated, but I knew the passengers would be as well. All three planemates filled with extremely angry people were brought back to the gate. My priority was to go to my office to catch my breath and to get a grip on the occasional harsh realities of the job. But before being fed back to the lions, I made the disheartening call to the gentleman who extended the invitation to me for that night. My illusions of grandeur again plunged to a record low. Respectfully, I kept him abreast all afternoon of the circumstances. He encouraged me to keep a positive attitude, but I knew the merciless *'indefinitely'* from the captain was analogous to; settle in for the night Claudia because you're not leaving any time soon. It was difficult enough dealing with the operational issues at hand, but then the planemate operators, who were already upset about having to wait for twenty minutes at the hardstand, returned everyone back to the gate and left. They are not required to wait for reboarding because of the high volume of demand by other airlines. After making my dreaded personal call, I had to control my anxieties and once again walk directly through the angry mob that were now back at the gate to get to the microphone...again!

My only recourse was to justify their anger which I did, and I profoundly apologized for the unexpected turn of events. I also tried to explain in German what a Transponder output tube was. As stated, passengers listen intensely because they demand the truth. Once they hear candid details, they assume a more benevolent attitude. They realize their safety is paramount, nor do they want a malfunctioning aircraft leaving a minute too soon. At 8:20 p.m., Delta successfully completed the transponder installation.

The three planemates were again summoned and I made a final announcement advising the passengers that this time they were indeed leaving, and I thanked them for their incredible patience. While they politely lined up and walked past me to reload, I sincerely expressed my apology to each one of them individually. Delays happen. It's par for the course. We've all been on the other side of the podium. The manner in which a delay is handled becomes crucial for an airline's reputation. After all the planemates were enroute back to the aircraft, I again went ramspide and up the stairs for a quick briefing with the captain as we waited for the load-sheet. As per his instructions, all three port aircraft doors were to be used to expeditiously enplane the passengers. They entered from the front galley, the mid-section and the rear galley to expedite boarding and everyone raced to their seats. As the handling agents and I dashed back down the starboard steps so the doors could be shut and the chocks removed, we sat in the car out on the tarmac waiting for that magnificent aerodynamic marvel to be pushed back. As always, the tremendous roar of the engines was exhilarating.

LT Flight 1553 was officially *"Off The Blocks"* at 9:00 p.m. However, while sitting in the car, I had to keep my cool to prevent an emotional meltdown. My colleagues knew about my evening plans and expressed genuine remorse for my socially aborted personal flight of fancy. They knew all too well the commitments and powerful highs and lows that airline staff must accept due to circumstances beyond their control.

On June 26, 1993, Luciano Pavarotti performed gratis at Central Park in New York. A crowd of 500,000 people was estimated to attend. Having been a guest at the 1990 FIFA World Cup--Three Tenors concert in Rome three years prior, I was elated to once again be in the presence of greatness. (Sidenote: The Rome concert was the first time all three tenors performed together.) My enthusiasm to share spit and sweat with 500,000 strangers at Central Park was not exactly enchanting. Fortunately, my date knew that I had this teensy little antisocial flaw. Therefore, he made arrangements for us to sit stage-front away from the madding crowd…. Thank you, Gideon! As a long-standing philanthropist and patron of the arts, his worldwide invitations were incredible.

After the Central Park concert, we were attending a dinner with Pavarotti and friends.. My final curtain call to stoically cancel with him was at 9:30 p.m. While dialing, I bit my lips to keep from crying. I calmly cleared my throat to maintain composure and told myself to be cool and not to go into a tizzy. Having anticipated the update, he answered the phone immediately. Like a little child, I started blurting out juvenile spasmatic eruptions such as I can't go, I hate my job, I'm quitting etc. until I ran out of infantile expletives.

He insisted that I just take the helicopter over to New York City, *'as is'* uniform and all, and we would just meet everyone in the restaurant after the concert. For a moment I contemplated it but by virtue of conventional hygiene, I despairingly declined. I was dishevelled and stunk from running around all day like a crazed lunatic trying to execute my perfect plan in an imperfect world in an industry where unpredictability was prevalent.

Whenever I had an important social commitment in Manhattan, my MO was to arrange for a comp room at JFK airport, then shower, change and take the helicopter to the city, which was gratis. I know that really sounds pompous, but it was my reality simply because of the perks of my job. I was able to work miracles at times but given that four-hour delay, it was logistically impossible.

In the illusive Shakespearean Forest from Shakespeare's Midsummer Night's Dream, the euphemistic Puck observed the behavior of its inhabitants: rational/erratic, good/evil, foolish/wise and in his final analysis, he so eloquently concluded, "What fools these mortals be." However, without dreams, hopes, adventures and passions, we merely exist and not fully live. For years, one of my aspirations was to sing a duet with Pavarotti. My family and I were raised with classical music and my operatic voice was inherent. Weeks prior to the concert, I had become ensconced in fulfilling my Midsummer Night's Dream that night and already visualized myself drinking the bubbly and clinking champagne glasses with the 'King of High C's' as we both sang *Libiamo*, the beautiful drinking song from the opera La Traviata. Because of the transponder setback, the only bubbly I experienced that night was from foaming at the mouth and from bubbles that burst, and the only party I attended was a pity party.

Having an analytical mind, I had to reconcile this cruel and unjust social deprivation, so I dug deep to understand the silly lesson or the meaningless moral that I was supposed to learn from this unrelenting day. I couldn't come up with much of anything other than, the next time an amazing opportunity presented itself... screw it, I was going! However, when my senses returned, I reflected on the extremes that airline staff were subjected to. It truly wasn't financial security but rather an addictive elixir distilled with paradoxical passions that set the airline industry apart from the mundane.

Before beginning my long after-flight paperwork, I stopped by the KLM lounge. How unusual, right? My overwhelming sadness was apparent, so my colleagues comforted me with generous offerings of verbal and liquid compassion. That particular flight day and night was indeed a compilation of my unfeigned, coexisting worlds. Shakespeare's Midsummer Night's Dream imparted relevance to my serendipitous tale from the tarmac, for it begged the question, must we always discern fantasy from reality, or can they harmoniously exist? We mortals have become so programmed to deny ourselves a parallel universe.

Surviving in an urban jungle with all its responsibilities *and* being given an opportunity to sing with Pavarotti were reflections of my essence. However, the urban jungle had priority that flight day, and with everlasting regret, my visit to the Enchanted Forest had to remain an unfulfilled, elusive fantasy.

Chapter 10

Look... Up in the Sky, It's a bird.

Written by Paul Brown and Narrated by

Lara Brown Bozik

As an aerospace engineer retiree, I would like to share the following true story regarding geese congregating on the airfield at our Long Island, New York facility. I hope you will find it as amusing today as it was back then.

In a frantic attempt to rid the airfield and runways of this dangerous problem, the airport manager purchased a device that he thought would be a surefire fix. Birds flying into aircraft windshields and engines have been a serious problem since the Wright brothers. Case in point: Captain Sullenberger's heroic landing on the Hudson River in 2009. This occurred because a flock of birds shut down both engines on a US air flight while airborne over New York. We all tried to find solutions to this ongoing problem in our engineering department since our fighter aircrafts were constantly being bombarded with birds and their poop. Subsequently, this caused major damage to the cockpit canopy.

When addressing the issue at meetings, the birds became known as UFFFs (Unidentified-*Foul*-Flying-*Fowls*). The ingenuity and the wisdom of that egghead department decided to construct an air-cannon to shoot chickens that were approximately the size of the UFFFs. The brilliant idea was met with rousing approval by all.

Keeping in the avian spirit, a gaggle (pardon the pun) of eager engineers descended upon local butcher shops to purchase deceased and plucked chickens. Upon delivery of this new miracle air-cannon device, I assigned a crew to install it on the runways. Several days later, upon inspection, I drove out to the airfield to see this gadget in operation. Well, the big day arrived. With the integrity of the windshield ready to be tested, the chickens were locked and loaded... ***BOOM! BAM!*** However, the featherless missiles struck with devastating results. The cheers and the proud back-slapping moments were halted. Unbeknownst to these gallant intellectuals, mangled chicken parts from the test firing graced front porches, roofs and eaves of neighborhood houses and splattered over half of Long Island. Needless to say, this half-baked UFFF project found its way to the aerospace company's 'dead file' bin real quick, never to be mentioned again.

Shortly after the cannon fiasco flop, a frantic second attempt was made to rid the airfields of the UFFFS. After the initial air-cannon debauchery humiliation wore off, subsequent research from a different viewpoint was conducted. The airport manager and his team of eggheads went out to eastern Long Island to visit a farmer who invented a gadget that prevented crows from feasting on his harvest. For all intended purposes, *this* gizmo was a surefire fix. Once again, the same cannon cohorts installed it with convinced certainty that the UFFF airfield problem would be resolved by ridding the birds from the ground.

Allow me to first describe the gadget: Picture, if you will, a two-foot-long aluminium tube with a fourteen-inch propeller attached to one end and a ten-inch propeller on the other end of the tube, which was mounted on stanchions by the side of the runway. The object being; one prop would spin clockwise while the other would spin counterclockwise. I can only say that after looking at this toy, I burst into a fit of laughter. Fortunately for me, I did not lend credence *or* my name to this engineering marvel. Once in operation, the birds reacted immediately, not by flying away but by nonchalantly sitting under this convoluted contraption, just chilling out! To add insult to injury, they were enjoying the cool breeze and the soft, soothing *whooshes* as the props gently lulled these happy little geese to sleep. If these UFFFs could talk, they would have requested a dozen more! Proving to be totally useless, it was removed a few days later and added to the 'dead file' bin along with the misfired air-cannon. Both ill-fated avionic projects *flew* the coop!

Chapter 11

Breaking the Glass Ceiling at JFK

Written and Narrated by

Dolores Lantt Hoffman

Rather than quitting my job at Pan American World Airways, I decided to take on a man's job. I was very happy being an administrative assistant in the cargo department, working for a man who truly appreciated my work. He left, and the position was filled by another man who resented him. I was a political leftover and not used to being treated so astringently. Being a teamster in Local 732, I had the privilege of bidding on any jobs that were posted as PAN AM always hired from within before going to the outside. Those were the days when one could climb a corporate ladder. Three months went by with no office job openings, and I was coming close to actually resigning.

Then, one day, five openings were posted for cargo service agents. I bid on this position which literally entailed unloading freight off trucks at the receiving dock. Despite being the most senior qualified bidder, I was called into the office by four of my bosses at the time. I was told by one of them that if I didn't pass my three-month probation, I would be out of a job, and as a result of having to lift very heavy weights, I'd probably never be able to have children. He also said that I would be the laughingstock of the airport along with other such derogatory remarks. I told them that they had to give me a chance to prove myself. With that said, they decided to send me to PAN AM's medical office for a medical exam. After spending over two hours there and then not finding anything medically wrong with me, the doctor sent a report saying that my physical stature was too weak to perform the job. When they came back to me with that remark, I told them that out of one hundred and fifty or so warehousemen, I could point out a few whose physical statures were as slight as mine. I only weighed 116 lbs back then. They had no choice but to finally award me the position. I knew how they worked, having typed a few previous disqualification letters for them to other women who tried to step into positions such as this.

I held my head high, I persevered, and I was determined and not willing to give up. My husband Ed was installing a tile floor in our dining room at the time, and he taught me the proper way to lift; stooping rather than bending with boxes of tile. Ed was and is so supportive and behind me all the way.

Since female uniforms did not exist, I had to purchase a male uniform. Ordering a man's shirt in size *small* was no problem, but for the pants to fit my hips, I had to go to a seamstress and have the uniforms altered to fit my body. Otherwise, they would have just fallen off my hips. Then when I reported to work, I was surprised by many of my co-workers who did not accept a woman in their warehouse. I just had to prove that I could do it and I sure did. In the year and a half that I worked on the dock, I embarrassed more men into doing more work than they ever had before. For example, I remember a box no bigger than 18 x 18 x 18 inches that arrived weighing approximately 300 pounds. One of the three men standing by me said let's go get a forklift to put it in a bin. PAN AM was the first airline at JFK with bins that were like little trolley cars on a track that went around the warehouse. I said to them, "are you kidding? There are four of us here! We can lift this into a bin." One of them said, "Oh yeah, let's just see you move it." With all my might, I prayed that I could, and I was able to slightly spin it around. Within about the next five seconds, they had it in a bin, the door closed and sent enroute in the system.

One day, one of the men intentionally ran over my foot with a piece of equipment. How immature of him. I grabbed the top of his arm and watched five streams of blood run down where my fingernails had pierced his skin. No one ever messed with me again. I remember someone on the dock signing for a shipment of baby chicks, of which a good number were unfortunately dead. Our shop steward said that it stunk too bad for his men to handle and they refused to palletize the baby chicks. Being the animal lover that I am, I called my husband Ed and asked if we could convert our dining room into a pen until we found out what to do with the remaining chicks. Right after that phone call, thank God, one of the managers came down and asked for volunteers to palletize them. I nudged Big George, one of the fellows that I knew would help me. He said yes, and we both volunteered. I had to hold my nose because the stench was horrible. However, we palletized the chicks, threw some netting over the pallet and off they went to South America. We saved as many as we could. After we were done, I walked up to Big John, the shop's steward at the time and said, "Did that smell too rancid for you and the boys to handle?" *He* became the laughingstock of the warehouse because the *girl* did the job!

Many jokes were played on me, including being locked in one of the bins with a co-worker and sent around the system until they finally let us out. The most memorable was the time I came down from having my coffee break with the girls upstairs. A janitor was briskly sweeping up the floor at the receiving dock. Not only were the dock workers there, but workers from the container station, from the palletizing station and from other areas of the warehouse. No truckers were at the dock at the time. I whispered to a co-worker and asked him what I missed. He said you didn't miss anything yet. With that said, I took a closer look at what was on the floor. A box of condoms had broken open and were all over the place.

In addition, some of them were blown up like balloons with faces drawn on them and taped to the wall of the dock. I didn't know how the words came to me as I looked at all of them straight in the eyes and said, "All these balloons and no party?" Very quickly, all of them went back to work. Not one had anything to say to me.

They never did put a ladies' room in the warehouse for me. In the beginning, I had to walk up two flights of stairs to get to it and then come back down. This got old very quickly, so I asked a trusting co-worker to stand outside the men's room, which he did.

Eventually, all the guys did it to save me the up-and-down ladies' room trips.

I remember one time coming back from lunch and there were truckers from all over the country lined up. They were not letting anyone unload their trucks because they wanted the *girl* to do it.

I became very strong and never turned down a job assignment. Having worked odd shifts, I would sometimes do my food shopping on my way home from work at 9:00 or 10:00 p.m. at night...even later. My husband reminds me of how I used to kick the door to knock because I had two large bags of groceries in each arm compared to carrying one bag at a time before this job. I truly thought of it as a free gym and kept myself in really good shape.

Nearing the end of that year and a half, I became very ill with a bad case of bronchitis. I had a dozen long-stem roses delivered to my home with a big card signed by all the warehousemen wishing me well. I treasure that card to this very day. That was a most endearing 'end result' of proving myself worthy in a man's world. As they say, *'you've come a long way, baby,'* and I surely did.

Shortly thereafter, I bid on a management position as a recruiter in the personnel department. After nine months in that position and one year before Delta took over PAN AM, I accepted a position as director of personnel for Evergreen Airlines. Then on to being the Airport matchmaker, also known as Program Manager for the Queen's (New York) Air Services Development Office, our acronym being ASDO. I was on contract with the Port Authority of

New York and New Jersey for the last thirty years, working at John F. Kennedy International Airport, retiring in 2021. I would not trade one day of my fifty-three-year aviation career with anyone for anything.

Today, my name appears in the PAN AM Museum Foundation's Hall of Fame for 'breaking the glass ceiling' in 1972 for *all* women. With perseverance, any of us can achieve whatever we put our minds to. Just go for it!

Chapter 12
The Ostrich Flight

Written and Narrated

by John Grasser

That's me! In the mid-nineties, when I was employed as a Station Manager at JFK for a major European airline, I got caught up in a feathered frenzy that shall remain with me until they throw dirt on my coffin.

I should start off by saying that we flew Boeing 747 'combi' aircraft into JFK in those days. A combi is an aircraft configured to carry passengers as well as cargo on the main deck separated by a wall because this area was heated the same as the passenger cabin and offers about 100 inches of height for shipments... 96 inches to be exact. We were able to move very large animals such as horses, chimps and the like, which was a very lucrative market for our cargo division. We even flew in a shark once, but that's a whole other story.

Well, one extremely cold winter day, I received information on a high-value shipment of baby ostriches that were due to arrive in a few days. If I recall correctly, the number was 150, with 25 per crate. They were coming in from Africa, transferring through Amsterdam and into New York. Now, we were constantly shipping baby chicks, and they were known to be quite sensitive to extreme temperatures. If it was too warm, they would perish due to the heat, and if it was too cold, they would freeze to death if exposed to cold weather for any extended amount of time. That meant the shipper would place a claim against our cargo department, and in turn, our cargo department would moan to me about crappy handling and not caring about their products… blah, blah, blah… you get the idea, right?

Now, the week the ostriches were scheduled to arrive was one of the coldest we had experienced in a long time. So cold in fact, that there were a few flights that had to return to Europe with the inbound freight on board because the cargo door was frozen shut, and we couldn't open it upon arrival at JFK. I'm talking in the low teens, single digits here in New York. Now, with my vast experience in dealing with baby chickens and knowing quite well about the high value of these ostrich chicks, I made the educated decision to delay them. After all, they were coming from Africa and must be protected against the cold at all costs. So, I telexed Amsterdam (no email back in the day) to hold the ostriches until I further advised before I left the airport for the day.

Returning to work the next morning, I received a rather long wordy telex, remember, no email, from none other than our senior vice president of operations advising me that under no circumstances should these ostriches be delayed any further. They were insured for one million dollars. The consignee in the States was screaming that he needed the birds, and a lawsuit was pending. He added that he didn't care how we got the birds into New York and off the aircraft, but we better get it done. And for a kicker, it was noted that these birds were growing at a rate of three inches a day. Growing three inches per day? I now had this cartoon vision of these poor birds with their little heads and legs sticking out of the crate and growing larger by the hour, and it was all my fault.

So, based on this love note from our senior VP, I had no option other than to have the shipment flown into JFK and offloaded in sub-20-degree weather. Calls were placed to our cargo department to make sure that the consignee was advised and ready to accept his damn ostriches. Plans were ready, and pre-meetings were conducted. All equipment was checked, and everything was in place. In such cases, specialized 16-wheelers are used to load the shipment directly from the aircraft onto the tarmac. They are equipped with rollers that are hydraulically raised and lowered to allow the shipment to roll easily on and off the trucks, but more on that later. I must add that the trucks were the responsibility of the consignee.

The time had come. The flight was heading west across the Atlantic. Our cargo department had brought the consignee over to the ramp with his two trucks, and a meeting was held. I found out that ostrich is the "new" beef, very lean and very tasty, easy to raise and that I should be seeing it in the supermarkets very shortly. Sure thing, I thought to myself, all I want to do is get these damn birds the hell off my aircraft without freezing them. We close the meeting in full agreement... i.e., the flight will arrive, the high loader will be positioned at the main deck door, the trucks will position, and the

93

birds will be offloaded. As Ed Norton, Chef of the Future, once told TV viewers, "Zip-zip, it's done."

We leave the office, me in silent prayer that the cargo door will open and not be frozen shut upon arrival. The new ostrich rancher brought along pallet plastic to wrap around the crates to protect the birds from freezing winds and the bitter cold. Good idea, I thought to myself. I tried to size up this fellow prior to the flight arriving. He looks like he's ready to have a nervous breakdown and seems to know very little about the birds he had most likely spent his life savings on by having them shipped in from Africa. Oh well, it's the "new" beef. He'll be fine.

The circus begins. The aircraft arrives at the gate, and the passengers start to deplane. We hold our breath until the cargo door begins to open. Step one is a success. The door opens, and I breathe a sigh of relief. Little did I know that would be the last time I breathed normally for the next hour… the next several hours! Have you ever wondered what 150 ostriches that have been penned up in crates for about five days smell like? I've been involved in many shipments with a good number of odorous animals. I have been subjected to the smell of horse shit, cattle shit, monkey shit, mink shit, dog shit, cat shit and an array of other shits. This shit took the cake! I wouldn't wish this smell on my worst enemy, well, maybe. I stopped breathing up there on the main deck. The thought of that ostrich shit entering my lungs was sickening. My scarf immediately went over my mouth and nose. (Side note: did you know that monkeys will throw their shit at you? Be forewarned.) So now the ostrich rancher is on the main deck feverishly wrapping his crates in pallet plastic in preparation for the offload.

The first two pallets of birds are on the loader being lowered to the truck that had been positioned. The first pallet started to enter the truck, but there was a problem. Remember those hydraulically controlled rollers that are raised in the truck bed to make an easy off/unload? Well, from what I witnessed, it looked as if they were not working. This is not the first time such a situation has presented itself. There is a procedure that can work, although not recommended for live shipments. But we have no choice. What takes place is that the first pallet is positioned at the truck door and then forced into the truck by the second pallet which is moved along by the loader, also hydraulically operated. All goes well… pallet one is in place. Now comes number two, which, of course, presents the problem as it cannot be fully loaded into the truck. So, the second pallet is partially forced into the truck by hand, and the truck slowly pulls away from the loader. Again, there is a procedure I have seen used on the ramp that has always made me cringe when initiated, and this time it's with million-dollar birds! I need to add that at this point, I am back down on the ramp, watching intently and trying to breathe normally.

The procedure that follows is that the truck driver slowly speeds up... remember that 'slowly' word? He then brakes hard, which in turn jerks the pallet into the truck. One attempt works a bit, the second attempt a bit more, and now, on the third attempt, the driver must have realized how to operate the hydraulic wheels and raise them. But this time, he elects to gun it forward, which in turn starts the two pallets of birds to roll backwards out of the truck. In all honesty, the second pallet was more than halfway out of the truck, bent almost to the ground before that jackass hit his brakes and catapults back into the truck. At that point, I was not sure if I was frozen due to the weather or out of fear for my life when the pallet started heading towards us. I also thought at that moment I might experience yet another new smell, that of the ostrich rancher's shit! Once the trucker figured out how to operate the rollers, the other pallets were easily loaded onto the truck and driven away.

The shipment is loaded and leaving the field, and the rancher looks exhausted from the ordeal. The cargo manager seems pleased it went 'OKAY'. Yeah, sure, and I am just happy to have it over and done with.

We all say goodbye and get on with our tasks, but I have one minor problem. My clothes, my shoes, my hair, and everything about me smells like ostrich shit. I can't shake it. I reek. Thank goodness that was the last flight of the night. I can go home now and sandblast myself. I ended up having to leave my clothes out in the garage for a good week before I could even take them to the dry cleaners. The next day, when I arrived at work, there was another telex from my senior VP congratulating me on the 'good' job. I started thinking... "Well, I better keep that thought to myself!"

As I mentioned at the start of this story, that was in the mid-nineties, and originally, it was told when we were closing in on 2011. We are currently in 2025. Allow me to ask, when was the last time you saw ostrich steak offered for sale in the meat section of your local market? I found it once or twice on a few restaurant menus; however, I could never get myself to order it because, more than likely, I knew that poor steak's grandfather.

I'll close with one final point. Years after the ordeal on an aircraft as a passenger, I was thumbing through a magazine and came across an advertisement for ostrich farming. There was a picture of a few of those dopey-looking birds standing in some pen in Colorado or someplace like that. What really caught my eye was that they were standing in about two inches of SNOW! Wherever they were, it must have been quite cold. Go figure! This fowl-smelling ostrich story was just another average day at JFK and another true tale from the tarmac.

Chapter 13

Do As I Say, Not As I Do,

Written by Former Aer Lingus Station Manager

Gerry Moore

So there I was, one frigid routine morning in 1965, on my way to Heathrow Airport for an 0700 shift. I was just tootling along the airport Rd. in my battered, sputtering old Morris Minor automobile, half-daydreaming and thinking of nothing in particular. The only notable event on my shift was the scheduled arrival of a Boeing 707 charter flight from New York at 0730, and I was the only Aer Lingus staff member on duty covering that arrival.

It was 0645, and I was almost there when, lo and behold, I saw a big Aer Lingus Boeing 707 taxiing across one of the airport overpasses a full 45 minutes early. Shit, shit, shit, I thought to myself as I raced to the office. I found out that the aircraft had been assigned a hardstand assignment, which is a remote parking spot, so I grabbed the keys of a ramp car and drove like the clappers to get there, hopefully before the aircraft did. I did get there just as it was being marshalled to its parking position. No jetways back then, folks, just ramp buses to take the passengers to the terminal. The engines shut down, the signal was given to position the stairs to the front passenger door, and the first bus pulled up to the foot of the stairs.

It was then that I saw, to my horror, that the ground between the bottom step and the bus was a sheet of ice. A major hazard to passengers and, of course, a potential lawsuit if any of them slipped and got hurt. Quick as a flash, I signalled the cabin crew to hold the passengers while I ran up the stairs into the aircraft to make an announcement asking the passengers to please be careful as they boarded the bus due to ice on the ramp. They waited patiently for my announcement, and then, on my instructions, they carefully followed me down the steps.

With a whole planeload of passengers watching and diligently following my instructions, I stepped off the bottom step and fell right on my ass on the ice, losing my uniform hat in the process to the cheers of the delighted passengers. Mortified, I picked myself up and went to retrieve my hat which by now was blowing across the ramp, completely forgetting, of course, about the ice.

Then, another resounding cheer went up from the delighted passengers as I went down to the ground for the second time. Needless to say, no further announcements were even contemplated!

Chapter 14
Lost and Found

Written By Rosa Kamel

Narrated by Lara Brown Bozik

My name is Rosa Kamel. At the ripe old age of 18 and just out of high school, I had been told by a friend of mine that Air France, or as we jokingly called it, Air Chance, was hiring temporary summer passenger service employees. I was lucky enough to be hired even though I did not speak a word of French at the time. This temporary summer job turned into full-time employment that lasted approximately seven years. I had many interesting and exciting experiences while working at JFK.

I shall never forget one particular incident. We handled an airline called Air Afrique. Upon its arrival, as well as for all international flights per se, one of the not-so-fun duties of a passenger service agent was to clear any suitcase that was not claimed by the arriving passenger. The reasons were that passengers would legitimately forget to pick them up in the excitement of coming to America, or they knew that they were bringing in something illegal and felt that at the proverbial 11th hour, they were going to get caught by U.S. Customs.

Well, that morning was indeed one of those flights where the latter applied. Approximately a dozen bags were unclaimed leftovers. In clearing the leftover baggage, we first had to get them opened with master keys for the various locks that these suitcases might have had. If that didn't work, we just clipped the locks off so Customs could view the contents. Well, on this particular 5:00 a.m. arrival and after the sixth or seventh suitcase, the routine process of opening them continued. They contained the usual dirty laundry, while some contained interesting items such as African wood carvings, ivory elephant tusks—illegal, of course, and other bizarre things that just never ceased to amaze me.

With each suitcase I opened, I thought to myself-- one man's gold is another man's junk, and how true that was. I came to one suitcase that had some tears all around it, and it looked pretty beat up. Although its exterior appearance seemed a bit odd, I, nonetheless, had to get it open. As I carefully unzipped the suitcase and flipped the top open, I almost went into cardiac arrest.

All I saw was a huge open mouth with very large teeth that instantly snapped at me. It was a baby alligator! My screams were heard throughout the building. A Customs officer came racing over to me as the alligator started crawling out of the suitcase. I stood there in total disbelief. Luckily, thanks to a quick-thinking janitor, he carefully put a big empty garbage pail over it and subsequently dazed our new JFK arrival until quarantine officers came, nabbed the African gator and took it to the JFK quarantine facility.

The passenger never did return to claim his frightening friend due to the fear of being fined and arrested for bringing in a live and dangerous animal without proper documentation, you think!! I don't know what happened to the baby gator, who by now must be fully grown and probably swimming in Florida lakes!

The normal procedure was that plain old unclaimed bags filled with dirty laundry were held for three months and then simply disposed of. The holding area was not a place you wanted to be any longer than necessary. If anything of major value was found, it was reported to the Port Authority. That storage facility must be quite interesting. And where does that stuff go after three months? To the eternal lost and found abyss?

My many adventures, such as this one, definitely made coming to work every day a unique and exciting experience. It surely earned its annals in JFK's history of Tales from the Tarmac.

Chapter 15

A Healthy Disregard For The Impossible

Written *by Henk Guitjens*

(|The following events occurred in chronological order)

How to make money when the world is on fire!

- *August 02, 1990*: Iraq invades Kuwait and seizes the oil fields
- *August 06*: The UN imposes a trade embargo on Iraq
- *August 07:* Saudi Arabia requests U.S. troops to defend them against a possible Iraqi attack
- *August 09:* First U.S. military force arrives in Saudi Arabia
- *August 10:* Saddam Hussein declares a "jihad" or holy war against the U.S. and Israel
- *September 14/15:* UK and France announced the deployment of 10,000 troops to the Gulf
- *January 12, 1991:* Congress grants President Bush the authority to wage war
- *January 17:* Operation Desert Storm begins at 3:00 a.m., Baghdad time.

On January 17, 1991, while attending a function at the Netherland Club in New York City at Rockefeller Center, the reception came to a halt around 7:00 p.m., when the news broke that the U.S. declared war on Iraq and that an invasion would be imminent.

As we were watching the news with our mouths open, we wondered what this would mean for the economy, the business at hand and for our future.

As Vice President and General Manager for Martinair Holland (MP), we were knee-deep in the process of launching a substantial charter and scheduled charter program from Amsterdam to multiple cities in the United States and Canada. Programs were printed, and agreements were made with the consolidators and the travel industry. The sales staff was busy selling the seats to the travel agents, and an advertising campaign had started. In 1991, Martinair was operating a convertible fleet with DC-10s and 747s.

As the cargo market historically was always stronger during the winter season, most of the aircraft were converted into a cargo configuration, whereas in the spring and the summer, passenger seats replaced the cargo floor. As per the planning, all Martinair cargo aircrafts would be converted in April 1991.

One can imagine when I returned to the office the next day since our staff was quite worried about this sudden development. The news channels were reporting on the imminent invasion, and the papers were full with the troop's deployments. The public, understandably, was becoming very concerned about this development and soon it became clear that many of them wanted to stay close to home.

Passengers began cancelling their reservations, groups were cancelled, and business travelers were holding back their plans to travel. Any new bookings had stopped, and the consolidators and tour operators were approaching MP to reduce the allotments.

One morning at the end of January, my phone rang, and the president's executive secretary said, "Henk, the Boss wants you to be at HDQ (Headquarters) at Schiphol by tomorrow." That night, I climbed onboard KLM 644 and flew to Amsterdam, as did other area managers of Martinair.

After I freshened up upon my arrival in Amsterdam, I met with Martin Schroder and his executive staff. He looked all of us in the eye and said, "I am cancelling the North American passenger program, except for Florida and the Caribbean, and I am converting the fleet into cargo!"

Then he said to me "Guitjens, I want to fly for the U.S. Government! I know that they will require a lot of cargo lift, and I do not believe that the U.S. carriers can supply enough airplanes." In response, I said, Martin, that will be difficult to do, as we are not a U.S. carrier, and we are not part of the **CRAF** (Civil Reserve Air Fleet) program.

Martin Schroder said: "I really do not care. Go to the Pentagon, the State Department, call the Dutch Ambassador in Washington, go to the **MAC** (Military Air Command) and get it done!"

He assigned the VP of International Affairs to the team, and we started to plan a visit to the various U.S. government departments. After several days, we were able to establish appointments in Washington and Scott Air Force base. After speaking to them, we quickly learned from **MAC** that many U.S. carriers could not supply enough airplane lift, and **MAC** was looking for a way to approach their allies and the European and Asian carriers.

In the meantime, we did a "dog and pony" show (impressive, notable presentation) in the USA as we spoke to several Generals and Colonels at the Pentagon and Scott Air Force base, trying to convince them to consider MP's cargo fleet. It was never done before: and there appeared to be great concern about a reaction by Congress, the complicated **CRAF** prerequisites, and by the U.S. carriers and their unions.

But MP had taken the initiative, and **MAC** became interested in talking to us. They quickly dispatched a team to Holland and visited KLM and MP (KLM, at that time, owned 50% of Martinair). They discussed Martinair's fleet, reviewed the financial records and maintenance programs and viewed the regulatory process.

MAC realized that MP could supply the additional lift and was a very reliable company. Our maintenance records were excellent and better yet, MP-owned American-made planes. Yet there was another complication: It was difficult for the U.S. Government to dispatch funds and payments to a foreign carrier. Also, there was not enough time to obtain waivers or permission since supplies and troops had to be moved quickly.

The payment issue was resolved whereby monetary donations of a foreign government could be applied for payment. Hence, it became a tripartite arrangement. MP could fly the cargo missions, the U.S. Government had made the agreement, and another government would make the payments to MP. In addition, the U.S. Government took over the war-risk insurance, and guaranteed the fuel supply.

When all the parties agreed, contracts were signed, and MP started flying for the US Government. It was mostly "sustainment goods" or cargo, as it was called, and about one hundred missions were flown from various U.S. Air Force bases to Germany and to the Middle East. At the same time, the U.S. Government used the Rotterdam harbor to bring large numbers of troops to Europe by naval ships. MP was hired to supply the catering upon arrival before the troops were dispatched by rail to Germany and flown to the Middle East.

The 1991 Martinair's annual report shows an FL75* (Dutch Guilders) million gross profit and an FL52 million net profit, an increase of 83% over the year of 1990. The flexibility, the vision of Martin Schroder and his staff, and adequately taking advantage of the changes in the world arena, has always served Martinair well.

It was a major effort by the MP's staff, inspired by MP's President and founder, Martin Schroder, who never took *NO* for an answer and always had a '*healthy disregard for the impossible.*'

Chapter 16

Airline Addiction

Written by John Mangano

Many people start out in other careers, but once they enter the airline industry, they become trapped in a lifelong addiction. 'Working the line' is very much like being in a love affair that involves extreme highs and painful lows. For those who are not members of this great family, they will never truly be able to understand that this love becomes an eternal partner, and that is so true.

I started out as a New York City ironworker. My job entailed walking steel beams 60 stories in the air with some of the best and bravest people you could find. You and your partner would work in tandem, each pinning his end of the beam with nuts and bolts and then walking the beam high above the clouds to the next one. One job I will always remember was installing the windows on the World Trade Center, 110 stories high in the sky. You could easily see JFK Airport from that spot high above New York City.

Then, one day, I got a call from a friend of mine who was the Station Manager of Northeast Airlines at JFK. They were having problems with their new computer cargo moving equipment that they were looking to contract on a permanent basis. He asked me if I knew anything about that type of equipment and if I could help him out. I told him that if it has a blueprint, the location is on the ground, and it's warm, I'm your man. He hired me on a trial basis as a consultant. I got the shock of my life as I quickly found out that the cargo airline business at JFK was the Las Vegas of the East: sin, sex and shoddy work were all entangled within a strong labor union. However, from the viewpoint of a brawny young ironworker who would try anything and didn't know fear, this sounded like an ideal assignment for me at that time.

On My first day at JFK, I drove out in my shiny Buick Riviera to meet with the airline cargo director and his staff. When I arrived, the guard at the facility told me that if I wanted to park close to the cargo building, I would have to pay a fee. Not so! But nonetheless strange, I thought, since I was there for a scheduled meeting. But what did I know? Thinking, okay, I guess that's the price of doing airline business. The receptionist told me that the director and his staff had left for lunch, and she was instructed to tell me to meet them at a nearby place called Jade East. I found the restaurant, sat down at the table and introduced myself. The waitress came over and said everyone was having a dingaling, which was a double bloody Mary. Wanting to fit in, I ordered the same.

The first thing the director said to me was, 'Fasten your seat belt. You have a tough job in front of you." Once again, I reiterated if it's on a blueprint, I can fix it.

That night, I was at the hangar for the midnight shift to meet the staff and the lead man of the shift. One of the workers told me that he was somewhere around. While I was waiting for him, I decided to check things out on my own and I walked around this state-of-the-art cargo complex. Needing to use the men's room, I walked into the lavatory and there I stumbled onto the lead man with one of the women workers engaged in a compromising position. I was quite embarrassed and said, 'Sorry to bother you guys. I see that your system is obviously in working order, but we must meet right now regarding the automatic cargo system problem." He was not the greatest help since when I asked him why the system did not perform and why it was out of service, his only response was, 'We needed to buy a new machine," and that was it. After his intelligent answer, my next step was to review the maintenance records and then watch the operation myself.

The machine operated automatically, retrieving items from bins and then delivering them to a tow line of carts for the truck dock. The recurring problem was that many times the machines were going to empty bins. This resulted in damage to the overall system. The first thought I had was that maybe this was more of a human problem than a mechanical one, so I installed a 24-hour guard on each machine. Well, much to everyone's surprise, the machines worked 24/7 without a breakdown!

It turned out that some workers were erasing the master commands from the machine's logic box and then placing bets among themselves on which cargo bin the machine would destroy.

Once the system was proven successful, the airline was elated; and not only did I sign an ongoing contract with the provider, but also, as a result, it provided me with additional assignments.

I found this airline business fascinating. Each day represented a new and different challenge. There was a sense of excitement, and I, like my colleagues, became a JFK junkie. I was addicted. The airline business got me, and there was no turning back.

Chapter 17

Airline Addiction

Continued

by John Mangano

Following my success in solving the problem with the automatic cargo system, my next assignment was to oversee the busing of airline employees to and from the parking lot to the International Arrivals Terminal. This may sound simple, but the logistics involved with scheduling drivers and setting up the necessary maintenance to keep sixteen buses operating around the clock at that time made it a challenging job. One incident stands out. We had several bus breakdowns, and in addition, an undue number of drivers were out sick. This resulted in long delays as airline staff had to wait for extended periods of time to get to their jobs from the employee parking lot to the IAT. Frustration finally boiled over when one frustrated airline employee took matters into his own hands. He climbed aboard a bus that was sitting there with no driver. He got behind the wheel, loaded the bus up with other waiting employees and drove it on his own to the terminal. He pulled up to the front entrance, parked it, walked inside to his job, and then called us to come pick up the stolen bus. He is now a manager at the airport, and to this day, he is known as the 'Jackie Gleason Bus Robber of JFK.' Just another day at the airport! You never know what is going to happen.

One thing you can always count on, however, is that whatever does happen will be unexpected.

Another unexpected event occurred when the Concorde SST first began flying into JFK. The airline scheduled a press conference to promote the SST service. The airline manager was tasked with developing a plan to move the Concorde from the tarmac over to the hangar where the press conference was being held. His plan included the strict provision that no one other than the service team of cleaners would be permitted on the aircraft while it was being towed to the hangar. However, he could not resist the temptation to ride along himself.

Once the Concorde towing was successfully completed, he had made prior arrangements to have a stair-truck meet the Concorde at the hangar so he could deplane because he was also in charge of the press conference. As the SST reached the hangar, the Port Authority police took control. For security reasons, they decided to lock down the aircraft and not let anyone off. So, you can imagine the humiliated manager's surprise when he was locked in. Well, needless to say, the schmuck missed his own press conference!

Now, JFK is not the only airport where the unexpected happens. It's endemic to the airline industry worldwide. It was the end of the day on a Friday when my duty manager came into my office and asked me when I had spoken last to the head of our operation at Boston's Logan Airport. I told him yes, that we had spoken earlier during our regular morning conference call. The duty manager told me that he had just gotten off the phone with him and that he was involved in an incident with a police car as he was heading home after a few drinks at the Cloud 9 Lounge at Boston's Logan airport. I immediately placed the call. He got on the phone and explained that he was driving home in his company car when the car in front of him, a police car, suddenly stopped and he hit it. I told him I would catch a flight from LaGuardia to Logan, and he immediately asked if I was coming to fire him. I told him no, but that I needed to hold a company hearing to determine all the facts about the incident. I took a shuttle to Boston that Sunday night at 6:00 p.m.

Believe it or not, he called me every hour all weekend long, asking again and again if I was coming up to fire him. He was at the gate to meet me when the flight landed, and I assumed I would be taken to a hotel for the evening. The first words out of his mouth were, and I'm sure you can guess, …are you here to fire me? I once again assured him that we needed to have a company hearing before any action was taken. He then proceeded to tell me that he had not secured a hotel room for me and that he was taking me to his house for dinner because he and his wife wanted me to sleep over. That was a bit awkward. His wife greeted me at the door, and the first words out of her mouth were—"are you going to fire my husband for hitting the police car with a baseball bat?" Well, she had spilled the Boston Beans.

He not only hit the police car with our company car, but he also then proceeded to get out of his car, walk over to the police car and smash it with a baseball bat for getting in his way. I guess he might have had more than one or two cocktails at the Cloud 9. Fortunately for him, since he was very well acquainted (connected!) with the local police, the charges were subsequently dropped. However, our company could not condone that type of behavior, so we were forced to let him go. Thereafter, he learned to control his bat-swinging activities.

Eventually, he formed his own airline service company, got a lucrative contract from Delta Airlines, from which he made a small fortune and is now happily retired.

As I said, you never know what to expect in the airline industry other than to expect the unexpected!

Chapter 18
Hijacking of PAN AM Flight 93

The following episode was shared and recounted to me by a dear friend, Ursula Goshen, who had been a Special Service Manager at PAN AM in the 1970s.

One day, while managing the usual passenger-related matters, Ursula was advised, with limited details, that a PAN AM 747 aircraft had just been hijacked. Back then, disseminating information was much slower than today, thanks to the ever-evolving high-tech world that makes media news readily available as it unfolds. She immediately began coordinating and processing incoming data to the proper system channels worldwide.

The hunger for peace in the Middle East has always been untenable. As a result, numerous political and military organizations were founded under the guise of equality. On September 6th, 1970, members of a Palestinian terrorist group hijacked *four* aircrafts, all on the same day and all bound for New York. Their mission statement was to get Palestinian guerrillas released from European and Israeli prisons.

The first two, a TWA flight from Frankfurt, Germany and a Swiss Air flight from Zurich, Switzerland, were ordered at gunpoint to land at Dawson's Field, which was an abandoned British Royal Air Force airstrip in the Jordanian desert. The terrorists dubbed this airfield their 'Revolutionary Airport.' The third hijacking was an EL

AL flight which originated in Tel Aviv with a stop in Amsterdam and then on to New York. This, too, was commandeered to land at Dawson's Field. To execute this well-rehearsed takeover, four terrorists were to board EL AL's Flight 219 together, but only two got through security.

Approximately 1/2 hour into the flight while over the British Isles with the hijacking already in progress, the flight attendants refused to open the cockpit door. They immediately advised the captain via an intercom at which point he put the aircraft in negative G-mode, causing a sudden drop in altitude. He also intentionally made a steep nosedive so the two hijackers would lose their balance and fall. Subsequently, the Sky Marshall killed one of them and with the help of passengers, he seriously wounded the other, who was a female…keep that in mind. A safe emergency landing was made at London's Heathrow Airport. The fourth hijacking was the PAN AM Flight 93.

When all four terrorists originally checked in for the El Al flight, two of the four were denied boarding at Schiphol Airport in Amsterdam because their counterfeit African passports had sequential numbers and that raised a red flag. The other two were cleared. The two that were bumped, one being an American citizen, decided to hijack Flight 93 instead. Aircraft hijackings were easily plotted back then because airport security and screening were still in their infancy stages. Up until 9/11, weapons were simply concealed and carried onto aircrafts. Flight 93 originated in

Brussels, Belgium, with a stop in Amsterdam enroute to its home at JFK. While on the runway and ready for take-off, the astute captain brought the aircraft to an abrupt stop.

He was suspicious about the two African passport holders and engaged them in conversation for a few minutes. It was then that the hijackers seized the aircraft, instructing the captain to head for Jordan. The quick-witted captain convinced the terrorists that he could not land at Dawson's Field because the new PAN AM 747 jumbo jet was too large for that airstrip. He was then instructed to fly to Beirut for refuelling, at which time several more hijackers boarded with additional explosives. From there, they were commandeered to Cairo, Egypt, where these terrorists had one of their headquarters. At 4:30 a.m., seconds before touchdown, one of the grenades had already been lit.

The passengers and crew were told by the hijackers that they had to exit the aircraft immediately because within 3 minutes, all the explosives would detonate onboard. According to reports, the in-flight director, who was the hero of that flight, and the crew deployed the emergency chutes and safely evacuated all 136 passengers in ninety seconds. At that time, this was the fastest-ever evacuation in emergency landings. The captain stopped the aircraft as quickly as possible out on the tarmac with no access to safety, and everyone just ran, leaving their belongings behind. Within one minute of escaping onto the tarmac, they watched in horror as the 747 exploded and burst into flames. Afterwards, the passengers were checked medically and psychologically, and they were taken to local Cairo airport hotels. A couple of days later, PAN AM ferried an aircraft to bring them back home to JFK.

Ursula, along with her colleagues, made the necessary distressed arrival arrangements. One of her tasks was to call a local department store, advising them that she and her co-worker would be there shortly to purchase amenities for the 136 passengers. Since the flight was arriving on a late Sunday afternoon, the stores were not anxious to stay open.

Ursula spoke to a manager of a big department store and asked him to please understand the tragic nature of the situation and he eventually complied and stayed open for them. They bought every pair of shoes, every kind of slippers, and anything that resembled shoes since the passengers arrived empty-handed and barefooted. They had nothing with them because they had evacuated the aircraft in Cairo two days prior via the emergency chute and SOP (standard operating procedures) mandated removing their shoes. The PAN AM staff assembled everything possible that they could find to give to them. Upon meeting the flight, they were handed out to everyone.

Ursula vividly recalled how dazed yet amazingly calm the passengers were until one little girl, approximately four years old, started crying and desperately started looking for her doll. That was the breaking point for everyone.

On September 8th, the passengers, whose final destinations had been Los Angeles and other various USA cities, were reconnected on flights and were given first-class seating. That day, they had once again been traumatized. While looking out the window at JFK airport and waiting for their connecting flights to bring them back home, another aircraft burst into flames for the second time in front of their eyes. A Trans International Airlines DC 8 was deadheading from JFK to Dulles Airport in Virginia. Deadheading is when an aircraft travels without passengers and has only crews onboard going from one city to another.

At take-off from runway 13R, the aircraft climbed to 300 feet, rolled to the left, crashed and caught fire, killing all eleven crew members onboard. According to reports, a piece of asphalt debris had entrapped itself in the aft stabilizer, which is on the tail of the aircraft and provides stability. September 9th, a fifth plane, a British carrier from Bombay to London, was hijacked. The terrorists plotted yet another empowering demand: the release of the female hijacker who was wounded in the failed EL AL hijacking and arrested upon the emergency landing at Heathrow Airport hours earlier.

The British aircraft was also permitted to refuel in Beirut and then commandeered to Dawson's Field to join TWA and Swiss Air. On September 11th, most hostages were released, except for flight crews and fifty-six Jewish passengers. On September 12th, all three empty aircrafts were blown up with explosives. On September 30th, with the help of the Jordanian government, the remaining hostages were freed. The various governments conceded to the hijackers' demands, which eventually afforded them carte blanche to execute more grandiose acts of terrorism. Hijacking was a valuable tool to stimulate publicity and gain recognition for a particular cause. This form of submersion eventually became child's play and transitioned from a political tool to a murderous weapon.

For Ursula and her colleagues, September 8th's afternoon morphed into September 9th's morning and continued indefinitely with no rest for the weary staff. Compassion cannot be measured in linear time. The staff humbly gave of themselves, for they knew their workload was so inconsequential in comparison to the terror and the anguish those brave passengers endured on TWA, Swiss Air, EL AL, The British Aircraft and PAN AM's frightful Flight 93....all on the same day, all bound for New York!!

Chapter 19
Tail 'IN' The Tarmac

Recounted by Timber

Due to the political turmoil in Iran both then and now, literary anonymity had been requested by an endearing friend who graciously offered to share with us events in his life that warranted concealing his identity. For the following three amazing stories, he shall respectfully and simply be referred to as Timber. He was, however, the antithesis of simplicity.

Circa 1957-1982

Timber was a Lieutenant Colonel and pilot instructor in the Iranian Imperial Air Force. In 1971, he was stationed at Hamadan Air Force Base in Western Iran before being deployed as an F5 fighter pilot to Vahtaati Air Force Base in Southern Iran, due to the conflict within Iraq. Northern Iran's climate and topography were cold and mountainous. However, Vahtaati AFB was in the sweltering desert. Flights were scheduled in the evening because of the intense heat and sandstorms, with daily temps averaging 120 degrees. This wreaked havoc on the pilots and the aircrafts since this AFB had no hangers for the F5s. Every two hours the pilots in 'full flight' equipment had to do cockpit rotations due to the intense heat. To avert heat strokes while sitting in the cockpit, they had to continuously pour cold water on their oxygen masks.

One evening, Timber received a 'Scramble Line' (priority in aircraft take-off) from the tower to scramble out at 7:30 URGENT. As a result of the two-hour rotation on this particular flight, Timber was the #2 wingman to the flight leader. Shortly after a 'cranked out' locked formation take-off (pedal-to-the-metal), he started drifting back and losing speed. According to Timber, the leader requested that Timber go to auxiliary-power, but he advised him that he was already on max and afterburners. He continued drifting back with the leader still ahead and then he quickly pulled away. He checked his instrument panel and realized the right engine wasn't putting out enough power. The leader said he'd follow him back and instructed him to bank left, circle and start the descent. Timber then made a shallow turn to land and maintained an altitude of 350 ft.

With much anguish, he put his landing gear down for final approach, and the a/c (aircraft) began dropping at an alarming speed. In such cases, instrumentation and flight controls work in reverse, known as ARC, (Area of Reversed Command.) At only 40 rpms, he calmly but desperately tried to restart the right failing engine. At zero power, it had completely shut down, at which point, the tower advised him to eject NOW!

Life-or-death situations are predicated on split-second avionic judgment calls on the ground or in the air with very little time to pray for divine intervention. With his life hanging in the balance, he had to make one of these life-altering, nano-second judgment calls... to bail or not to bail. True to form, the Iranian Indiana Jones chose the latter for two logical reasons. One was that he felt a sense of loyalty to try and save the a/c, and the other was the fact that he was very frightened about ejecting because he knew the problems many pilots had encountered with the ejection seat on that particular jet fighter. There were reported incidents by his NATO F5 pilot colleagues where ejection seats had malfunctioned. The manufacturer, which we all know, refused to acknowledge the harrowing defects. As a result, many pilots were killed or crippled.

The ejection seat mechanisms on the F5 usually caused instant death because the breakthrough canopy device was located on the top back of the seat just behind the captain's helmet. It was a sharp spike with a point on top of it that purposely shattered the canopy so the seat could eject. However, the device would embed itself into the pilot's spine by going downward in lieu of upward. Horrific scenarios flashed through his mind; to either eject with the probability of being a vegetable in a wheelchair or die should it malfunction. For Timber, both would have been a death sentence or as he told us-- to just hold on tight to the stick and brace for impact. There was no choosing the "lesser of two evils" because both options sucked. True to form, he braced himself, held on for dear life and purposely crashed his F5 on final approach at a speed of 135 knots an hour (155 mph).

Upon the initial impact, the a/c broke into three sections as it hit the ground with the nose up. The nose, which contained the ammunition (50 Caliber rounds) and oxygen apparatus, immediately caught on fire in front of him. He could hear the ammunition detonating only 15 feet away as he sat trapped in the cockpit. The tail which contained the fuel broke 10 feet behind him. While still harnessed in the captain's seat, he was saturated with fuel when the seat started tilting right at a 90-degree angle. His left leg got stuck in a hole *in* the tarmac that was caused when he crashed. As a result, his left leg stayed in place while the seat and his trapped and bloodied body keeled over. The visual is analogous to a mighty tree toppling over while the root remains firmly planted in the ground, hence the nickname *TIMBER*.

He vividly remembers the sound of all the bones in his left leg being pulled in half and shattering while being drenched in fuel with the nose 15 feet away still ablaze. He attributes the tail not exploding due to extreme crosswinds which blew the fumes away from the cockpit. He laughed when he said, "Boy, I was lucky... I would have been shish kebob on a six-foot skewer. It was really hot, and then I lost consciousness."

He had no recollection of the rescue, only what he was told by the ground crew who saved his life. Since Timber crashed only 10 feet short of the runway, it enabled them to rescue him immediately. The crew used a ladder to pull him out of the cockpit and improvised by using it as a stretcher. They also told him that when he was placed on the ladder, his entire left leg was dangling in mid-air and hanging by a thread.

The AFB hospital was only half a mile away from the crash site. Due to the highly trained rescue efforts of the ground crew, he regained consciousness despite his burns and agonizing injuries. While regaining consciousness in the emergency room, his maverick mindset was intact, and he found it quite amusing that the young macho doctor on duty that night was watching The Sound of Music in the AFB theater. The Julie Andrews groupie was astounded when he saw Timber's severely mangled body and immediately called for a backup of 5 additional surgeons. The shoulder harness on the ejection seat had cut so deeply into his shoulder and neck that the doctors felt he would die due to total blood loss. The surgeon and his team prevented him from bleeding to death by aggressively stitching up most of his neck and right shoulder. One month later, he was released from the hospital, never to be the same again.

The debilitating pain, wounds and permanent scars did not slow him down any longer than necessary. As a true aviator, Timber bit that bullet, spread his wings and once again took his rightful place in the F5 and the esteemed 'First' seat!

Chapter 20
The One And Only

by Timber

From 1978 to 1982, Timber was the Pahlavi Imperial family's (Shah of Iran) Personal 747 pilot. Among the Shah's many opulent spending sprees under the guise of national security, he had purchased sophisticated radar equipment from a well-known U.S. electronic firm, which I was asked not to disclose. The Shah requested to have this equipment flown directly from the U.S. to Iran without it being public knowledge.

To do so, he purchased several used 747s from TWA and had them converted strictly to carry cargo. Boeing was most happy to accommodate the Shah since, as Timber regaled, 'Boeing was discreetly paid astronomical figures in good old U.S. Dollars.' However, despite his wealth and purchasing power, the Shah faced a major air-time impediment analogous to Isaac Newton's first law of motion: what goes up must come down and, in this situation, sooner than later! TWA arranged a clandestine monetary rendezvous with his royal highness, Mr. Pahlavi. The truism that money talks and bullshit walks is not just a euphemism…it is simply politics at its everyday core level.

McGuire Air Force Base in New Jersey to Tehran was 12 hours of actual flight time. The Shah's request to reconfigure the a/c from pax to cargo dropped the fuel weight to increase the cargo capacity. However, that further limited the 747's performance.

With a max fuel load, i.e., total fuel consumption for taxiing, take-off, in-flight, holding and landing, the 747 was three hours short. Just to reach a cruising altitude of 33,000 ft., this aircraft required 60 thousand pounds of fuel. Therefore, to fly nonstop MAFB/Tehran, a solution to the three-hour flight time shortage had to be found. The one and only answer was in-flight refuelling.

Amir Fazli was a lieutenant general commander at the Air Force Base in Tehran. This was the only person's name that Timber disclosed in his compendium for Tales From The Tarmac. I asked him why, to which he nonchalantly responded," He's fucking dead!" He felt all the other prominent individuals in his tales except Fazli and the Shah should remain anonymous along with his own identity for fear of political and criminal reprisal at that time.

The Shah was aeronautically astute since he had been a seasoned pilot himself and owned a fleet of private a/cs. The two men had a very good rapport. Timber not only flew the royal family around in their decadent Imperial 747, but as a personal favor to the Shah, he trained the Pahlavi's son to fly during his tour of duty in the Imperial Air Force. General Fazli knew that Timber's avionic efficacy was just what the Shah needed to resolve the McGuire/Tehran long-range fuel shortage dilemma. There was only one man for the job: Timber! He would be the first pilot in aviation history to refuel a 747 in mid-air. This became known as the Tanker/Receiver Project.

Subsequently, he was sent to JFK for six months, where he attended TWA's flight training school via the simulator, which was his first introduction to flying the 747 all-cargo a/c. There were a few snags of course that he had to contend with. Since the aircraft had been purchased by the Shah, they were the property of Iran, but they flew under TWA's flag to conceal the covert operation. To deter any suspicion, he had to wear the TWA flight uniform as well. He laughed while telling us this story because the in-flight crews really took a liking to him but would always ask him... are you an *ARAAB*? That remained a non-disclosure issue!

Timber was a young, good-looking stud with the demeanor and profile of an Iranian Indiana Jones, and he was eye candy for the 747 flight attendants. It was fun watching Timber's facial expressions as he humbly regaled, 'They all wanted a part of me, and a good time was had by all... a really, really good time!" No one expected such a young hottie to be flying a 747, which was the purview of seasoned 747 pilots. After completing his JFK training, Timber was sent to Seattle, Washington for more intensive training where he eventually got his Tanker/Receiver Certification. He then returned to Tehran to train Iranian 747 pilots to refuel mid-air.

Not knowing that the Shah owned the TWA 747s and based on an in-depth cost analysis study, the U.S. Govt. determined that utilizing 747s for the project was not monetarily feasible, and they felt using smaller a/c's to accomplish the same goal would be more cost-effective. However, the Shah clearly insisted on the 747 since its long-range cargo capability was the reason he purchased them in the first place. He also knew that the 747 was at that time, the fastest subsonic cargo a/c on earth at Mach.92 at a normal cruising speed of 682 mph. Mach 1 is 767 mph.

Once again, the dollar spoke even louder than before since the Shah was not going to scrap the project after already paying for all the radar equipment, the 747s and training, etc. Magically, the U.S. Gov't agreed contingent on the Shah footing the bill with crispy green '*cash only*' instructions. Obscene amounts of cash were flown into the U.S. from Pahlavi's endless fortune and as per instructions from the Imperial palace, Timber had to deeply line greedy pockets and heavily grease outstretched palms to people in the US.

The one and only actual 747 refuelling began over Nantucket, Massachusetts when he was 45 minutes airborne at 22,000 ft. A KC-135 tanker a/c belonging to the USAF hovered 15 ft. above his 747 and 10 ft. from the tail. Timber said he could see the whites of the KC crewmen's eyes; that's how close they were. A solid flexible hose locked into the nose of the 747 from the KC tail, and the successful refuelling took 30 minutes. As he explained, a boom operator is the tech man o/b (onboard) the KC that deploys the boom (hose) out of the rear of the KC tanker. He negotiates the actual transfer from the KC to the 747, aka male/female receptor. Upon completion of the fuel transfer, the KC disconnects, and the 747 then flies to its cruising altitude. Timber laughed when he said that during the refuelling, he and everyone smoked their cigarettes. The refuelling process was repeated in Spain via another USAF jet. Again, after 30 minutes at 22,000 ft., Timber cruised back up to 39,000 ft. and headed home to the Shah's kingdom. The total flight time from McGuire AFB in New Jersey to Tehran was 13 hours.

Upon landing in Tehran, all the engine lights were illuminated like a Christmas tree. This 747 cargo aircraft's oil usage could not exceed 11 hours of flight time and for whatever reason, miraculously, it did. Since only fuel could be replenished mid-air, not oil, it was a no-go for any future tanker/receiver flights. The USAF cancelled its commitment, labelling the reason "Sensitive needs of the 747-oil usage."

I do not profess any sympathy at all for the royal family losing billions of dollars since it was literally only pocket money and a mere spit in the ocean for them anyway. Eventually, Pratt & Whitney and Boeing modified the a/cs by making them shorter and faster, using less fuel and oil.

On a personal note, Timber and Debbie surely warranted a book of their own. Their stories of survival before and during their marriage were incredible. Considering Timber's outrageous accomplishments, he never demanded respect; he just commanded it. They were both loved and so admired by everyone, including by Jack and I.

Chapter 21

Eggs-odus

by Timber

Home is where the heart is, or so they say, but at what price? Timber loved his country as any good citizen would regardless of the corruption and leadership. His childhood memories of his close-knit family who lived in Iran for generations were loving. However, what he proudly considered a beloved homeland became one of imprisonment and punishment. In the latter part of 1982, three years after Debbie and the children left for the U.S., he made a most difficult decision and that was to flee Iran knowing he could never return.

He knew the dangers involved if he were to be caught, but the risk factors at that point in his life were secondary. Had he been captured, he surely would have had a backup plan since his attitude was that there are more ways than one to skin a cat. After methodically plotting, he seized the moment when the opportunity presented itself. The Empress, Farah Pahlavi, the Shah's wife, frequently went on shopping sprees via one of their Imperial toys, the 747 which along with Timber was at her beckoned call. It was nothing unusual for him to fly all over the world for the Pahlavi's nonsensical whims. One day he received orders from the Imperial Air Force to fly to Paris for the Empress to pick up curtains that she had ordered.

As absurd as it sounds to us, it was their norm. Tehran to Paris round trip was 10 hours of flight time. The costs incurred for each flight were ludicrous. In addition to fuel, landing fees had to be paid. Timber underhandedly had to dish out 2000 U.S. dollars and pay bribes on the tarmac so he could just walk into Operations, get his manifest, and fly right back out. On this particular trip, as he picked up the cargo manifest and read curtains and a pair of boots for the empress, For Timber, the insanity reached its peak shortly after that.

In 1979, The Shah and his family were forced into exile by the Islamic revolutionaries. They first went to Cairo, then they came to the U.S.! Life as Iranians knew it under the Shah's regime was a dichotomy. There was terrorism, but not blatant. There was wealth but not apportioned. Having dual citizenship was normal and people were free to come and go. Women were not mandated to veil their faces or drape their bodies in public. Socio-economically, the Shah did some good for Iran's infrastructure. Also, the Pahlavi mindset was more secular as opposed to the fanatical theocracy that killed innocent people since the beginning of time, all in the name of religion. Many friends like Debbie and Timber, as well as my sister and my nephew, lived in Tehran for many years during the Shah's rule and subsequently under the equally corrupt Khomeini regime.

My family in Iran was empowered monetarily and socially, but that ended immediately after the Shah was overthrown. Everyone's life changed for the worse, but the worst was yet to come. For Timber, it was time to flee. After the transition, Khomeini's

Revolutionary Guards ordered Timber to pick up eggs in Amsterdam, but not for breakfast, mind you. His mission on the 747 was to pick up 130 tons of eggs per day for 17 consecutive days under the pretense of feeding the nation that the Shah had impoverished. Other flights on a 707 flew from Tehran to Paris every day for beef. Nothing much fazed Timber anymore because of all the craziness he had already witnessed in his life.

He was thoroughly shocked when he saw that the daily pallets containing the 130 tons of eggs at Amsterdam's Schiphol airport came from Israel via EL AL Airlines. While laughing, he said "How about that… Jewish eggs feeding Iranian revolutionaries? You gotta love it!" Just prior to his 14th egg flight, an Intel officer who was a good friend and an informant told Timber that the mullahs were secretly getting into his files. The same mullahs had already killed several of Timber's colleagues, so he had to be extremely discreet in his stealth-like escape that would take place within a few hours.

The first officer on that 14th egg run flight was a loyal Khomeini sycophant who was assigned to surreptitiously follow and observe Timber. Timber had already checked out the flight, prior to the actual pre-flight briefing, i.e., information regarding the weather, his flight plan, etcetera. He knew he had to remain cool as a cucumber in that cockpit to stay alive and carry out his plan while still airborne. He calmly told the first officer to file an alternate flight plan to Frankfurt, Germany, just in case the weather conditions for landing in Amsterdam were too severe. ATIS: (**Air Terminal Identity**

Services) is comparable to our NOTAMS (**N**otice **to A**irmen) in the Western world.

It is a radio frequency in the cockpit that gives potential hazard and landing information to airmen. Timber told the first officer that he opted to bring the aircraft down in Frankfurt due to the heavy rainstorms in Amsterdam. ATIS clearly advised him that Frankfurt Airport had an equally low ceiling, (inclement weather.) When the first officer realized that he was heading for the runway in Frankfurt, he said to him, 'What the hell are you doing?' Timber knew that the first officer had a loaded gun.

Timber quietly landed the aircraft, parked it on the tarmac without saying a word, and calmly waited for the stairs so he could deplane. Once again cool as a cucumber, he walked out of the 747 and inwardly cried… *'Free. I am free, just keep walking and don't look back'* while anticipating a bullet in his back. The First Officer never expected him to abscond in public. Timber was even honorable enough to walk into Operations and order an alternate captain.

He left his cherished homeland with a calloused heart, the flight suit he had on his back, his standard flight bag, and $500 in his pocket, which is all he was allowed to take on any given flight anyway.

The next day he went to the American Consulate under emergency circumstances to come to America. At that time, Russia was fighting in Afghanistan, and as a result many Afghanis tried to flee to the U.S. President Carter mandated that anyone trying to leave regardless of their country, had to be cleared by the State Department. Otherwise, it was a no-go. Timber pleaded his case, stating that his wife and children were already in America. He certainly couldn't tell them that 24 hours earlier he absconded from Iran. They told him to keep checking back intermittently should there be any new State Department directives. However, no one gave him a time frame. He was faced with many other challenges as well such as where to go and what to do. He knew he had to go into hiding and that he had to count every penny since there was uncertainty as to how long he would be forced to remain underground.

He discreetly discarded his Iranian flight suit and somehow had to procure money to buy clothes and to pay off people who might potentially help him secure passage to the U.S. since that was his priority. He was cold, hungry, alone and homeless. There was no longer an Iran to which he could profess allegiance as he had done all his life. He recalled eating only Bratwurst on a stick, which is comparable to a hot dog, (but much better) several times a day from street vendors, since that was all he could afford. One of those Bratwurst encounters paid off for him. Timber had just finished his meager meal while sitting on the steps in front of a building. A stranger sat next to him, having a quick lunch on the go. In retrospect, he had often wondered if it was coincidental. The polite man struck up a conversation with Timber, and he introduced himself as a doctor who worked at the local Frankfurt hospital. They conversed in English, and during the course of the conversation, the doctor came to realize that Timber spoke Farsi, which is the Iranian language. Inwardly he questioned; was the impromptu meeting a stroke of luck after forty-five days in hiding? The doctor told him that a patient of his needed someone to translate Farsi into English since neither spoke the other's native language. The doctor was most willing to pay handsomely for someone's services but up until that point, he had not found anyone who could go to the hospital to sit and translate. At first, Timber hesitated but finally agreed, knowing that it might be his ticket out of Germany one way or another. So they arranged to meet shortly afterward in the patient's room, and once again, Timber had to crank up the old cool-as-a-cucumber routine when the alarming introduction was made.

The patient was an acute opium addict who had serious drug and legal entanglements with the law. As a result of his severe addictions, Timber said the addict's wife would sneak huge amounts of opium into his hospital room and he'd smoke it all in a heartbeat. When she was forbidden to carry anything into him, out of desperation, the junkie begged the doctor to roll some dope in cigarettes, and he would be generously rewarded because money was no object.

Needless to say, the doctor said no. Timber was not really surprised about the low-life condition of this addict since opium grows wild all over Iran. As my sister once said, it grows like crabgrass through cracks in cement sidewalks. The shocker For Timber was not this man's addiction but rather who he was. Timber's life once again flashed in front of him with an overwhelming threat of being captured after he'd come so far from oppression and so close to freedom. This despicable addict was a loyal Khomeini bodyguard and a close relative of Khomeini's Secretary of Agriculture.

Fortunately, Timber never disclosed anything about himself after the Shah's exile, nor did he do so in Frankfurt. He quickly just took the money owed him by the doctor and calmly said Aufwiedersehen Herr Doktor, which means goodbye doctor in German. With money now in his empty pockets, Timber went back to the consulate two months later and showed that he could pay for a ticket. The consulate approved and issued him a travel voucher which had to be presented at the airport upon check-in. He humbly requested an ID 90 industry ticket which is a payment of only 10%, and he got it from Lufthansa Airlines. He laughed as he *slowly* elongated the words to Jack and I: "I had one skinny, shiny dime left in my pocket by the time I got to Atlanta, Georgia."

When the aircraft left Frankfurt, Germany and started climbing, he asked for a cup of tea. He quietly sipped it while doing mental and emotional housecleaning. Some things he saved while other things had to be discarded like painful shoes that were loved but just kept hurting. And he cried. As his profound existence in Iran ended, and his new life was soon to begin, Timber humbly whispered to himself...*freedom is eight hours away!*

Chapter 22
Fast forward

by Debbie and Timber

Tucked in the breathtaking Blue Ridge Mountains, ninety miles north of Atlanta, Georgia is a little town called Helen. This hidden jewel is a replica of a Bavarian Alpine village in Germany. Brightly colored gingerbread shops and houses line the cobblestone streets with locals dressed year-round in their traditional German dirndls and lederhosen. Debbie from good old Brooklyn, NY and I, along with my sister Edith, have been friends since we were fourteen years old. Even though our lives eventually took different paths, we remained in one another's hearts. We all married, divorced, remarried, relocated, etcetera.

After many years of sacrifice and hard work, Debbie and her former husband Timber, who you now know from our stories, built a second home in Helen. Jack and I were honored when we were asked to be their first guests. The house, secluded high atop a mountain was beautiful. The host and hostess were extraordinary, and our times together were precious. After dinner, we would sit out on their back porch with a bottle of wine and candlelight to enjoy nature in its southern glory. Knowing both their fascinating history, it was the perfect time to ask favors of good friends, that is, to make literary contributions to Tales from the Tarmac.

They graciously accommodated my intrusive questions and I began scribbling notes with only the flame of a candle as a source of light and a bottle of white wine. My beloved and fun husband Jack used to say while snifting the glass of wine…' it's impertinent and malolactic' as he jokingly emulated white-wine snobs. Debbie would pretentiously agree with Jack, and we'd all be entertained.

As Timber began reminiscing, he started laughing and asked us if we wanted to touch his screws. A bit baffled, we had no idea what he meant until moments later when we saw the hundreds of screws that protruded through every inch of his left leg, along with massive scars from head to foot on his fatigued body.

He had been externally hardened by harsh realities, yet his teddy bear demeanour was indicative of a sensitive man who was faced with moral ambiguity throughout his life. Despite his 24/7 pain, which was second nature to him, he shrugged it off so matter-of-factly and had a great sense of humor.

Timber's wounds ran deep physically and emotionally. Debbie said there wasn't any one place in and on his body that wasn't damaged. Debbie herself…Mrs. Indiana Jones, also endured impassioned scarring. Her survival skills and tenacity were complimented by her brilliant mind, genuine kindness and extraordinary courage and coping skills during her horrendous ordeals while living in Iran due to the Khomeini regime's empowerment.

Listening to their unbelievable stories of resilience before and during their marriage was nothing short of amazing. Being with them and sharing time and tales was truly a privilege and an everlasting honor.

Conclusion

After many months of burning the midnight oil, I again thank my granddaughter Aleah, who took the front cover photo of the book in 2011 while we sat on the tarmac in Bermuda.

Also, the *Acknowledgement* and *About the Author* audios were recorded by a dear friend, Justin Conway. Justin is an Actor of Screen, Voice, Stunt performance, a Ninja Warrior and founder of 'World Ninja Sport', a successful international company…www.justinconway.com.

I humbly extend my heartfelt thanks to my family, friends and former colleagues for their ubiquitous and unique contributions as well as to all airline staff worldwide who have ingratiated themselves in my book and in my life, on the ground and in-flight!

My daughter Lara, thank you for your fun contributions and for being my biggest fan… I sure am yours!

My sister Edith, thank you for your IT and proofreading help.

My brother Steven, thank you for your on-going support.

My brother Eric, where are you?

My grandchildren, thank you for bringing me such pride and joy!

In addition to being family, I cherish our endearing friendships!

Ira…once again, here it is!

And to our listening audience, it was a *pleasure* sharing our tales from the tarmac with you. Along with my fortuitous narrative faux pas, we hope you enjoyed the revision from paperback to audio!